(801)
277-8328

DICTIONARY
OF THE
JEWISH RELIGION

DICTIONARY
OF THE
JEWISH RELIGION

DR. BEN ISAACSON

Edited by David Gross
Preface by Rabbi Saul Teplitz

PUBLISHING, INC.

DICTIONARY OF THE JEWISH RELIGION
Copyright © 1979 by Bantam Books, Inc.

Published by arrangement with Bantam Books, Inc.
SBS Publishing Co., Inc. Information address:
14 West Forest Avenue, Englewood, New Jersey 07631

ISBN 0-89961-002-1

LIBRARY OF CONGRESS
CATALOG CARD NO.: 79-67485

      Isaacson, B.
         Dictionary of the Jewish Religion.

      Englewood, NJ.: SBS Publishing Co.

      224 p.
      7912   790914

Photo research by Vincent Virga

Printed in Israel by Peli Printing Works

0 9 8 7 6 5 4 3 2 1

The Bible is not the sole basis of our religion, for in addition to it, we have two other bases. One is anterior to it, namely, the fountain of reason. The second is posterior to it, namely, the source of tradition.

Saadyah Gaon

Preface

by Rabbi Saul Teplitz

The Jewish religion is a subtle, challenging, and complex way of life. In the words of the prayer book, it is a "tree of life for those who grasp it." A book devoted to defining the basic words and phrases of the Jewish religion, as well as concepts and philosophies, for Jews and non-Jews alike, is therefore a welcome addition to the growing popular literature of Jewish interest.

One of the greatest authorities on medieval Hebrew literature was the late Professor Israel Davidson, of the Jewish Theological Seminary. In his will, read at his own funeral service, he wrote: "Do not eulogize me. To those who will study my books a hundred years from now, I will be as much alive then, as I was to those who studied them yesterday."

The greatest gift one person can give another is the gift of hope. Hopelessness leads to helplessness. We Jews, alone among all people, have managed to overcome defeat and surmount despair. When all hope seemed to be gone, Jews invented new hopes. To be Jewish means never to give up, and never to yield to despair. A great Jewish moralist of a past century taught that "Man must criticize himself and praise his fellow man."

If we want to discover the treasure of the Jewish faith, we must first find the old roads and dig them. We must examine the bequests of our Jewish past, reverently but critically. It is never either/or—either the past or the present but both in behalf of the future. If we live only in the present, we are anchorless, for to scrap the past is to pauperize the present. If we live on in the past, we tend to become irrelevant.

The great scientist Luther Burbank demonstrated that the cactus and plants similar to the cactus grow burrs solely in self-protection. So it has been with the

Jews—nation after nation, from the time of Haman onward, has sought to annihilate the very name and identity of the Jew from the face of the earth. But we have grown our burrs for self-protection and preservation, and those burrs are in the form of Jewish unity.

Only the casual Jews can bring about casualties. We must live as if all Jewish life depended upon us. The earliest mention of the Jewish people in non-Jewish records is found on the monument of Meneph-tah, more than 3,000 years ago. The inscription says "Israel is wasted and his seed brought to nothing"—and yet, when Frederick the Great was asked for the most convincing evidence of the existence of God, he declared "The survival of the Jew."

The Jewish religion teaches that in every age and to every man God addresses the same question: "Where art thou?" The final test of our lives will be not how much we have lived but how we have lived. Life is measured in deeds, thoughts, feelings. What is important is not luxury but love, not wealth but wisdom, not gold but goodness—this is the quintessence of the Jewish faith.

The Hebrew word for man, *adam*, can be derived from *adamah*, or earth, and from *d'mut*, which means the image of God. Man can become a worthless animal or a servant of God. Man is never final—he is always on the way. Man is not born perfect but perfectible. Judaism teaches there are forces within us that urge man to rise to higher planes—and there are forces tempting him to sink to lower spheres.

Religion has not been tried and found wanting—it has been found difficult and therefore not tried. Religion is not an escape from life, it is life. Religion was given to us so that we might truly live. True religion is not only the creed we profess, but also the life we live.

Israel's Supreme Court recently involved itself in the age-old question as to "What is a Jew?" This question has vexed definers for centuries. In the dictionary of the Portuguese language, a Jew is described as "a swindler." In the old Webster's dictionary, the verb "to jew" is defined as "to bargain or to cheat." Jean-Paul Sartre said "A Jew is a man who is considered by other men to be a Jew."

There is something about the Jew that is beyond comfortable delineation. We are the only people in the world tied to a religion, and the only religious group tied to a land. To live as a Jew means to live in two dimensions—the spiritual and sociological. We are tied to God through our religious faith and united as a people with the land of Israel as the focus of our peoplehood. In other words, to be a Jew means to live vertically in relationship to God, and horizontally in relationship to the Jewish people. These two aspects of Jewish life are one and inseparable.

In the divine symphony of the universe, we are compelled to declare, "Who am I? Nobody. It is God. He is everything." We Jews have a hundred different names for God. God is Father, Friend, Master of the Universe, King of Kings, and He is also "Du" (in Yiddish, the familiar form of You), and always God of Israel.

God is also referred to as "Makom," which means "place," because there is no place on earth where He is not to be found. Every field has the power of His breath upon it. Every hill has His stars shining over it. The atheist says, "God is nowhere"—the believer says "God is now here." We tend to forget that we are creatures of the Creator, and we are incomplete without Him.

The Jewish malaise, attributed to the loss of spirituality in the Jewish home, was cited by Franz Rosenzweig, the famous Jewish philosopher of the early part of this century. Judaism, he said, had become an "empty purse—formal religious education is of no avail in the absence of the reality of religion: a religion seen with the eye, tasted with the mouth, heard by the ear, in short, practiced physically." A homeless Judaism quickly becomes a hopeless Judaism.

In the 1960s, a new ideology arose—instead of "man's inhumanity to man," we now have man's immunity to man. Man simply ignores his brother. George Bernard Shaw once wrote that the "worst sin toward our fellow creatures is not to hate them but to be indifferent to them." Judaism has long taught that fear, jealousy and hatred can be quickly aroused, and can spread by their own momentum, but we must learn to love our fellow men because of ourselves. A

AARON. Brother of Moses, the first High Priest, and the progenitor of all priests (Kohanim). He died in the wilderness, on Mount Hor, at age 123, after officiating in the holy of holies for four decades. Rabbinic tradition emphasizes his love of peace and exemplary life of piety.

AARON BEN ELIJAH. 14th-century (c.e.) Karaite theologian who sought to give a philosophical basis to Karaite beliefs. His *Etz Hayyim* ("Tree of Life") was a response to Maimonides' *Guide for the Perplexed,* insisting that the Torah could never be altered or added to by oral law.

AARON BEN JACOB HA-COHEN. Born in France in the late 13th century, he lived mostly in Majorca, following the expulsion of Jews from France in 1306. He wrote the code *Orehot Hayyim* ("Paths of Life"), comprised of rituals and customs, which was later abbreviated. The shortened version, *Kol Bo* ("Everything's in It") became very popular.

AARON BEN JOSEPH THE PHYSICIAN. Karaite scholar who lived in Constantinople where he wrote an early Hebrew grammar and commentaries on the Bible. He introduced poems by Hebrew poets of Spain into the Karaite liturgy.

AARON BEN MOSES HA-LEVI OF STAROSELYE. Hasidic Rabbi of the Habad movement, who pressed for the introduction of emotions into daily prayers. He also wrote commentaries.

AARON BEN SAMUEL. 17th-century German Rabbinic author whose principal work, *Beit Aharon,* includes all references to the Bible found in the Talmud and in major post-Biblical literature.

AARON BERECHIAH BEN MOSES OF MODENA. 17th-century Italian mystic, best known for his *Maavar Yabbok,* which deals with burial and mourning laws.

AARON HA-LEVI OF BARCELONA. Spanish Talmudic scholar (late 13th to early 14th century), author of *Sefer Hahinuch* ("Book of Education"), enumerating the Bible's 613 commandments, and explaining them according to Rabbinic tradition. The book was translated into Latin and French.

ABBA. (Hebrew for literally "father.") Honorary title conferred on some of the Tannaim and Amoraim. Maimonides equated it with the title Rabbi.

ABBA MARI BEN MOSES HAYARHI. Talmudist in late 13th to early 14th-century who led a group of Rabbinic scholars in southern France opposed to philosophical and secular studies espoused by Maimonides' followers. Wrote *Minhat Haknaot* ("Zeal Offering"), containing Jewish scholars' correspondence dealing with controversy over Maimonides.

ABBAHU. 3d-century preacher who led the Rabbinic academy in Caesarea. Known for his modesty and coining of homiletic phrases ("The world exists through the man who effaces himself"). Highly respected by the Romans, he issued a decree that Samaritans should not be excluded from the Jewish community.

ABBAYE. Babylonian Amora who stressed importance of physical labor. Worked his small farm at night so as to be free to study during the day. Among the first Rabbis to differentiate between literal and exegetical interpretations of the Bible.

ABBREVIATIONS. (*Rashei tevot* in Hebrew.) Talmudic and Rabbinic works to this day make extensive use of acronyms and abbreviations, often shown by dots, strokes, or double strokes over an initial letter of a word, with the balance of the word removed. Examples of abbreviations abound: Tanakh (Torah, Neviim, Ketuvim) represents the three major sections of the Holy Scriptures (Old Testament).

ABLUTION. Washing the body, usually for a religious purpose. Total immersion in the mikveh is one example. In ancient times, the High Priest immersed himself (tevilah) before conducting the Yom Kippur service. Jewish law requires partial ablution (washing of the hands) before partaking of a meal, on awakening, and after leaving the washroom.

ABOAB. Family of Jewish origin in Spain. Born a Marrano in the 16th century, Immanuel Aboab reverted to Judaism, strove to prove the veracity of oral law. Isaac Aboab was a Talmudic scholar, author of *Menorat Hamaor* ("Candlestick of Light"), a collection of ethical Rabbinic teachings arranged by subject that won wide popularity among Jews in the Middle Ages. Isaac de Fonseca Aboab, a Rabbi in Amsterdam at age 21, led Sephardic Jews to Brazil in the 17th century, becoming the first Rabbi to officiate in the western hemisphere.

ABOMINATION. (*Toevah* in Hebrew.) Applied to something utterly despised on religious grounds, e.g., eating of unclean animals, idol worship, belief in magic, or use of false weights and measures. Seven examples of abomination are listed in Proverbs: a proud look, a lying tongue, hands that shed innocent blood, a heart that devises wicked imaginations, feet that run to mischief, a false witness, and sowing discord among neighbors.

ABORTION. Little known in ancient times. Biblical law stipulates that an attack on a pregnant woman resulting in an abortion calls for monetary compensation, provided "no harm follows" the attack. Otherwise, the attacker must pay a "life for life." The Talmudic commentaries, noting that it is not permissible to murder one person in order to save another, agreed that a woman in "hard travail" (thus endangering her life in the birth-giving process) should be saved and her unborn child destroyed— but not if "the greater part" of the infant has emerged from the womb, for then it is considered a person, and the woman's life may not be saved by destroying the child. Some Rabbinic commentators would permit abortion if the birth of a child would cause the mother to lose her sanity; others would allow it if the child would be born seriously deformed or an imbecile. Still others permit abortion where pregnancy is the result of rape, expecially the rape of a married woman. Abortion is not permitted for economic reasons or where the mother simply does not want to have the child.

ABRAHAM. Considered the father and founder of the Jewish people, the first of the Patriarchs, and the first man to espouse monotheism. Male converts to Judaism are generally called sons of Abraham. God made a covenant with Abraham, promising to make him father of a mighty people with a special relationship to the Almighty. The sign of the covenant is the circumcision of all male Jews.

ABRAHAM BEN DAVID OF POSQUIÈRES. Talmudic scholar in 12th-century France, known as Ravad. The leading interpreter and arbiter of Jewish religious law of his time. He opposed codifications and religious dogmas on grounds that they were inimical to the spirit of Judaism, preferring instead study of and recourse to Talmudic sources. Wrote commentaries, and a work on family purity; noted for his commentary on Mishneh Torah of Maimonides.

ABRAHAM BEN MOSES MAIMONIDES. Maimonides' son. He led the Jewish community in Egypt in the 12th and 13th centuries, serving also (like his father) as physician to the caliph. One of his best-known rulings, which remains in force, prohibits an individual Rabbi from excommunicating a member of the community.

ABRAVANEL, ISAAC BEN JUDAH. Leading Biblical commentator, philosopher, and communal leader of the 15th century who tried but failed to prevent expulsion of Spanish Jewry in 1492, through intercession with Ferdinand and Isabella of Spain. He found refuge in Italy, and through his prolific writings indicated an imminent Messianic era, thus buoying up the spirits of tens of thousands of Jewish refugees from Spain and Portugal.

ABRAVANEL, JUDAH BEN ISAAC. Son of Isaac Abravanel, he was an Italian poet, philosopher, and physician. His best-known work, written in Italian and published posthumously, is *Dialogues on Love,* in which he sought to define spiritual and intellectual love.

ACADEMIES. Schools for the study of Bible and the oral law. Such academies existed at Yavneh, Lydda,

Abravanel

Pekiin, Bnai Brak, and other sites in the Holy Land. Other academies were set up over the years, among the most famous of which were those in Sura and Pumbedita in Asia Minor. Other centers of study developed in north Africa, Spain, Italy, the Rhine region, and, still later, in eastern Europe. Since the destruction of European Jewry in the Nazi era, the two great centers of Jewish study are located in Israel and the United States.

ACCENTS. Signs used in the Biblical text to show sentence structure and give cantillation instructions (*taamei hamikra* in Hebrew). The accents are believed to have been included around the 8th century, but one tradition holds that they were given to Moses on Mount Sinai but forgotten until revived by Ezra the Scribe. Since the scroll of the Law that is read aloud at synagogue services has neither vowels nor accents, the reader is required to study beforehand in order to be able to read the prescribed texts accurately.

ACCIDENTS. Jewish law developed liability laws, dividing them into four principal categories: injuries caused during normal daily activities; injuries caused by something stationary; accidents that occurred on an individual's private property; and consequential damage. Accidental manslaughter in Biblical times brought in its wake exile to a city of refuge, where the perpetrator had to remain until the death of the High Priest then in office.

ACOSTA, URIEL. 16th to 17th century religious skeptic born to Marrano parents, who settled in Amsterdam, converted to Judaism, and then attacked Rabbinic Judaism, insisting that only the literal reading of the Bible was authentic Judaism. He was excommunicated, recanted, renewed his attacks on Rabbinic teachings, and was excommunicated again. Again he recanted, and was subjected to flogging and public penance. He committed suicide after writing autobiographically of his spiritual quest. Several modern novels and plays have been based on his life.

ACROSTICS. These are found in the Bible and in the prayer book, in the latter case often based on the author's name.

AD MEAH V'ESRIM SHANA. (Hebrew for "until 120 years.") Expression of good wishes used on birthdays, derived from the sixscore years lived by Moses.

ADAFINA. Sabbath dish, comparable to the east European cholent, containing beans, meat, peas, and eggs. It indicated to agents of the Inquisition that the household where such food was prepared and consumed was Jewish.

ADAR. Sixth month of the Jewish year. It usually falls in March. The festival of Purim falls on the 14th of Adar. During a leap year there are two Adars— I and II.

ADLOYADA. Purim carnival, nowadays usually featuring masquerades, in which celebrants are expected to be joyous enough not to be able to distinguish between Mordecai and Haman.

ADON OLAM. Hymn of uncertain authorship from

the 6th or 7th century, citing God's unity, timelessness, and providence. Sung at conclusion of the Musaf service in most rites, it is also recited by some while leading a bride to the bridal canopy.

ADONAI. (Hebrew for, literally, "my Lord.") One of the names of God. Because the name is considered holy by religious Jews, they substitute Hashem ("the Name") in everyday usage, pronouncing "Adonai" only at prayer or during the reading or study of the Bible.

ADOPTION. In Jewish religious law, adoption is not considered as binding as it is in Western civilization. An adopted child cannot, for example, inherit from an adoptive father if the latter dies intestate. In modern Israel, however, the rights of an adopted child have been legally protected. A non-Jewish child adopted by Jewish parents must be converted to Judaism individually. Rabbinic teaching held that raising an orphaned child was a meritorious deed, but saw this as foster rather than adoptive parentage.

ADRET, SOLOMON BEN. 13th-century Spanish Rabbinic authority known as Rashba, who served for 40 years in Barcelona as the leading spiritual guide of his time. His thousands of Responsa covered every aspect of religious, family, and civil law and had a marked influence on the subsequent codification of Jewish law. He was a staunch defender of Maimonides and opposed excessive mysticism. Although he did not oppose secular studies, he forbade students to pursue them until after the age of 30, stressing the importance of Jewish religious studies.

ADULT. Rabbinic law teaches that at the age of 12 years and a day, a girl was to be considered a *naarah* ("maiden"), and six months later she was to be considered an adult. The age of 13 was cited in the Mishnah as the age at which one was responsible for fulfillment of the commandments. The age of 13 years and a day is the generally accepted point at which a young man attains his majority. The age of 20 is cited by the Bible as suitable for ablebodied men to enter military service. Recent Rabbinic rulings in Israel have raised the age of consent for marriage for a girl to 16 years and a day.

ADULTERY. One of the Ten Commandments proscribed adultery, interpreted as sexual relations between a married woman and a man other than her husband. If properly witnessed, the crime carried the death penalty for both parties. An offspring of such a relationship is considered a *mamzer* ("bastard") and may marry only a fellow *mamzer* or a convert. Adultery, incest, idol worship, and bloodshed may not be committed even if the alternative is death. Rabbinic teachings prohibit sexual relations between a married man and a woman other than his wife, but do not define such a relationship as adulterous.

AFIKOMAN. Piece of matzah, taken from the middle of the three matzahs at the Passover seder, and to be eaten by all those participating in the ritual at the conclusion of the meal. It is customary for children to hide the afikoman, and refuse to produce it until after they are promised a suitable reward, thus making conclusion of the seder possible. This is done to interest the children and involve them in the seder.

AGGADAH. (Modern Hebrew for, "a legend.") Referring to the Talmud and Midrash, the Aggadah consists of material unrelated to Jewish law such as homilies based on Bible tales, stories, folklore, aphorisms, and legends. Some of the Aggadah material preserved in the Talmud and Midrash was originally passed on from generation to generation by word of mouth, and formal transcription is believed to date from the 5th century. Popular collections of Aggadah material include *Ein Yaacov* in Hebrew and *Tz'ena U're'na* in Yiddish.

AGNOSTICISM. Although Judaism and agnosticism are incompatible, some Jewish religious thinkers cite the revered Maimonides, who wrote, "Man can comprehend the fact that he [God] exists, but not his essence." Saadya Gaon, stressing that men should concentrate on intellectually manageable issues, taught that the human mind could not fathom the concept of the divine.

AGRARIAN LAWS. Although all Jewish religious laws must be observed worldwide, those that deal with agricultural matters apply only to the land of Israel. Operating on the principle that the Holy Land belongs to God, these laws provide for certain restrictions for offerings to the early priests and Levites (who did not in the main pursue manual labor), as well as for the benefit of the poor. The laws included leaving gleanings and a corner of the field for the needy, allowing the soil to lie fallow in the seventh year, and a ban on mixing two or more seeds in a fruit orchard. The fallow soil provision, called shemitah, is still observed by strictly Orthodox Jewish farmers in Israel.

AGUNAH. A woman who is not allowed to remarry because her husband has abandoned her, or because he is believed to have died but there is no certifiable proof. A number of Rabbinic reforms have been instituted in recent years to alleviate this situation for the woman's benefit, but they are not conclusive.

AHARONIM. (Hebrew for, literally, "the latter ones.") Term describing Rabbinic authorities since the 16th century, although in some cases the dividing line for the early ones (Rishonim) is the 12th century.

AKDAMUT. Special prayer recited in most Ashkenazic synagogues on the holiday of Shavuot, the feast of weeks. An acrostic poem written in the 11th century, it is both a reply by Jews to their persecutors and a promise of a blissful future.

AKEDAH. The dramatic story described in Genesis of Abraham's agreeing to bind and slay his son, Isaac, in accordance with God's command, and the subsequent substitution of a ram in place of the child, has remained to this day a lesson for the Jewish people—of unquestioning obedience of God's commandments, and readiness to become martyrs if necessary to protect the sanctity of his name. The Akedah story is included in the Rosh Hashanah service.

AKIVA. Rabbi Akiva, who lived in the 1st and 2d centuries, and who was illiterate until he was 40, had a marked influence on development of Jewish religious law, and arranged the oral law of the time according to subjects, thus laying the groundwork for the Mishnah. A patriot as well as scholar and Bible commentator, he was an ardent supporter of Bar Kochba in the latter's revolts against the Romans. Rabbi Akiva was arrested for continuing to teach Torah (despite Roman edicts to the contrary) and executed in Caesarea.

AKKUM. Term used in Rabbinic literature to describe one who worshiped stars or constellations; therefore, an idol worshipper. The term was coined to indicate the vast difference between those who followed other religions and pagans.

AL CHET. (Hebrew for, literally, "for the sin.") Recited on Yom Kippur (except in the concluding service), this community confessional lists a wide variety of transgressions, and asks for God's pardon on the holiest day of the Jewish year.

AL HANISSIM. Special prayer inserted in the services on Purim and Hanukkah, extolling God for his miracles that led to these festival celebrations.

ALBO, JOSEPH. 15th-century philosopher in Spain whose *Sefer Ha'ikarim* ("Book of Principles") is still studied today. He taught that Judaism was constructed on three main pillars—divine existence, divine revelation, and reward and punishment.

ALEINU. Prayer that proclaims God's sovereignty over the Jewish people and the whole world. It is included in all three daily and holiday services (morning, afternoon, evening). In the Middle Ages this nearly 2000-year-old prayer was censored by Christian clerics who mistakenly interpreted sections of it as insulting to Christianity. Medieval martyrs recited it as they were led to execution.

ALFASI, ISAAC BEN JACOB. Major 11th-century Talmudic scholar who founded a yeshivah in Spain. His *Safer Halachot* ("Book of Laws"), dealing with 24 tractates of the Talmud, was the most important Jewish religious code until it was replaced by Maimonides' *Mishneh Torah*.

ר׳ יצחק אלפסי הרי״ף

נולד ד׳ תשעג נפ׳ ד׳ תתסג

Alfasi

ALIYAH. (Hebrew for "ascent"; the same word is used to refer to immigration to Israel.) "Call-up" to the Torah reading portion of the synagogue service, restricted in most cases to male Jews aged 13 and up. (In recent years, as a result of feminist pressure, some Conservative synagogues have begun to give an aliyah to women, too.) Those called to the reading of the Torah are generally honored by a special blessing, referring to them by their first name (in Hebrew) followed by the father's name.

Alkalai

ALKALAI, JUDAH. 19th-century Serbian Rabbi and early Zionist. He learned of growing Balkan national movements, and in 1834 published a pamphlet urging Jews to return to the Holy Land rather than continue to wait for divine redemption. The religious Zionist movement regards him as an early forerunner.

ALMEMAR. Raised platform in the center of the synagogue upon which stands a table where a scroll of the Law is placed for public reading of Biblical sections. In more modern synagogues the desk for the scroll of the Law is combined with the platform in front of the holy ark. Among Ashkenazic Jews the almemar is also known as the bimah.

ALPHABET. The Hebrew alphabet, consisting of 22 letters, reads from right to left and is derived from ancient Canaanite script. There are no capital letters; five letters change form at the end of a word. Yiddish and Ladino are written in Hebrew letters, with some modifications, especially for vowel sounds. Greek, Latin, and Cyrillic alphabets are used in adaptations from the Hebrew.

ALROY, DAVID. 12th-century pseudo Messiah in the Caucasus and Kurdistan areas of Asia Minor. Although his first name was originally Menahem, he changed it to David to stress his proclaimed link with King David.

ALTAR. Low structure on which sacrifices were generally offered. The Bible's first mention of an altar occurs when Noah built one after the Flood had subsided and only he and those saved in his ark were left to repopulate the world. The Israelites who exited from Egypt and wandered in the desert for 40 years carried a portable altar made of wood.

AMALEK. Ancient nomadic people who lived in the Sinai Peninsula. They carried out a treacherous attack on the Israelites, who were on their way to Mount Sinai to receive the law. Since then the name Amalek has been used to describe any archenemy of the Jews. The final annihilation of the Amalekites will come, according to tradition, only after the advent of the Messiah.

AMEN. (Hebrew for "so be it.") Found in various Biblical texts, it is generally recited at the end of a blessing at a public service, or by someone hearing another offer a blessing. Christians and, to a lesser extent, Muslims, have adapted the word for their services.

AMIDAH. Also known as the *Shmoneh Esreh*, the 18 blessings, this section of the ritual is found in all daily, Sabbath, and holiday worship services. The word means "standing" and this prayer is recited silently and while the worshiper is upright, in effect becoming a "private" prayer to the Almighty in the midst of a public service. In many synagogues a worshiper who completes the recitation of the amidah may be seen symbolically taking a few steps backward—as though he had just left the presence of God.

AMORA (pl. AMORAIM). Rabbinical teacher during Talmudic days who interpreted for the populace. The Amoraim carried on their work primarily in Babylonia and Palestine; among the famous academies where they taught were those in Tiberias and Caesarea in Palestine, and Sura and Pumbedita in Babylonia.

AMOS. One of the Minor Prophets, he remonstrated against the moral corruption of his generation, warning of a day of judgment unless the people were sincerely devoted to the will of God. According to Talmudic interpretation, Amos's dictum "Seek me and live!" summarized the whole of Biblical teaching.

AMULET. Object worn as a charm to ward off evil, sickness, misfortune, etc. Amulets were worn for many years in the Middle East, and keep being unearthed in modern archaeological discoveries. Amulets are still worn by some sections of Jewry, and were used to a limited extent by some east European Jews in the 18th and 19th centuries, under the influence of growing interest in the kabbalah.

ANGELS. Judaism emphasizes man's direct link to God, without the need for intermediary celestial beings such as angels. Nonetheless, there are some references to special categories of angels whose job it is to fulfill divine instructions. In folklore, the angel of death (*malach hamavet* in Hebrew) is particularly well known.

ANI MAAMIN. (Hebrew for "I believe.") The 13 principles of faith as promulgated by Maimonides, recited in condensed form in many synagogues at the conclusion of morning services. Jews in Nazi concentration camps sang the words of the penultimate principle to a slow tempo, expressing their eternal faith in God and in a Messianic era. The song is a popular melody today in all communities.

ANIMALS. Judaism traditionally provided concepts

Angels depicted on a *drukermarke*, a printer's mark.

of kind treatment of animals, with laws designed to prevent torture, cruel treatment, and overwork. Sabbath rest, for example, includes domestic animals. A bird's egg may not be removed from the nest while the mother is present. Rabbinic law does not oppose vivisection for medical research but proscribes the infliction of unnecessary pain on the animal.

ANOINTMENT. Biblical custom of dedicating kings and High Priests by pouring oil on their heads as part of ceremonies of inauguration. The Messiah (*mashiach* in Hebrew) literally means "anointed one."

ANTI-SEMITISM. Hatred of and hostility to Jews and Judaism has a long history. In the Book of Esther, Persia's prime minister, Haman, refers to Jews living in the country as "a certain people scattered abroad and dispersed among the people in all the provinces of the kingdom, and their laws are diverse from all people, neither keep they the king's laws, therefore it is not for the king's profit to suffer them."

APIKOROS. Rabbinic version of the Greek name Epicurus, the philosopher who preached concentration on the pleasures of life in this world, since the soul and body both end at death. Heretics and non-believers were lumped together in Jewish tradition under the term "apikoros"—a designation still in use.

APOCRYPHA. Books not included in the Hebrew Bible (Old Testament) but included in Roman Catholic and Greek Orthodox canon, and dating to the period from the 2d century B.C.E. to the 2d century C.E. Among the works in the Apocrypha are Maccabees, Tobit, Judith, and Wisdom of Solomon. The original Hebrew or Aramaic of the texts is lost; only translations are extant.

APOSTATE. Jew who has voluntarily abandoned Judaism for another religion. Although an apostate in Jewish law is still regarded as a Jew, he is considered to have lost any privilege accorded to members of the Jewish community. He is known in Hebrew as a *mumar* or *meshumad*. The term has a pejorative connotation. However, a Jew who has been forcibly converted to another faith is never referred to as an apostate. Rabbinic authorities wrestle with problems today such as whether a Jewish wife, whose former husband has chosen to convert to another religion, still requires a *get*—a religious divorce—since he is technically no longer a practicing Jew.

ARAMAIC. Early Semitic language closely identified with Hebrew; small sections of the Bible (Ezra and Daniel) are written in Aramaic. Some of the major liturgical works are also in Aramaic, e.g., Kol Nidre, the Yom Kippur eve service, and kaddish, the mourner's prayer. Huge sections of the Talmud, both the Babylonian and Palestinian, as well as works of Jewish mysticism, are in Aramaic.

ARBA KANFOT. Known also as *tallit katan,* or a small tallit. A special garment worn under the outer clothing by male Orthodox Jews during the day, which contains the tzitzit or fringes at four ends, as prescribed in the Bible. The garment and its fringes are meant to remind the wearer to "remember and do all my commandments and be holy unto your God" (Numbers 15:39–40).

ARBA KOSOT. Four cups. Refers to the four cups of wine to be drunk at the Passover seder service.

ARBITRATION. Jewish law expounds the concept of arbitration, with the Talmud stating that to "effect a compromise is praiseworthy." A Rabbinic Bet Din (court) is used today in religious disputes, and is sometimes preferred by Jewish litigants in civil disputes. The court's decisions are considered final. Bet Dins in most western countries consider disputes in accordance with prevailing local legislation, making their decisions enforceable by civil judicial bodies.

ARON HAKODESH. Shrine or closet in the synagogue in which the scrolls of the Law are kept (they are removed during services for public reading). Found on the eastern wall in most synagogues (facing Jerusalem), the ark of the law (as it is usually translated) is often beautifully designed and decorated. A curtain in front of the ark is called a parochet; the ark is generally on a raised platform (*bimah*), and the *Ner Tamid* ("eternal light") usually

19th-century Galician Torah ark.
The ornament shows two phoenixes surrounded by
floral designs signifying the tree of life.

hangs overhead. When the scrolls of the Law are removed from the ark, and when they are replaced, the congregation rises.

ARTIFICIAL INSEMINATION. Most Rabbinic authorities prohibit and condemn the practice mostly from fear of the consequences of legalizing it. The consensus is that a generation of children whose true fathers would be known only to the attending physicians would lead to all types of ills, including the possibility of incestuous marriages. An exception to the rule is artificial insemination by the husband, which most religious authorities permit.

ASCETICISM. Since Judaism does not look upon the body as inherently evil, the concept of self-inflicted austerity as a form of expiation of past sins is unknown, with the exception of fasting. Celibacy is a practice opposed in the Bible, which calls for fruitfulness. Nonetheless, all through Jewish history there have been periods in which a yearning for an ascetic form of life was expressed. The most famous ascetics in history are the Essenes, who lived in the time of the Second Temple. Mystics who sprang up in the 16th and 17th centuries encouraged some forms of asceticism, some of which have been retained by Hasidic teachings, despite that movement's emphasis on joyous communion with God. Most Rabbinic teachings have stressed the need for leading a life of moderation.

ASHAMNU. (Hebrew for "We have sinned.") Opening words of the Yom Kippur prayer, listing 24 sins in alphabetic order, recited communally so that the entire congregation in unison recalls the past year's transgressions, and as a group prays for forgiveness. The prayer is generally accompanied by symbolic breast-beating.

ASHKENAZ. (Ashkenazi(c)—loosely speaking, Germany/German.) Ritual customs and prayers are generally divided among the Ashkenaz and Sepharad (loosely, Spain) communities. The former encompass primarily Yiddish-speaking Jews from central and eastern Europe (and their descendants in the U.S., Israel, etc.), while the latter take in Jews originally from the Mediterranean region, e.g., Spain, Portugal, Italy, Greece, Yugoslavia, Bulgaria, who developed their own "Jewish language," namely Ladino, a mixture of Hebrew, Latin, and Romance languages, contrasted with the Yiddish of the Ashkenazi Jews, which is close to German with additions of various Slavic and Baltic languages, depending on where Yiddish was spoken. Both languages retained a strong base of Hebrew and both were written in Hebrew characters, with slight variations for vowels. Jews from Yemen and from some other Asian countries are generally referred to as oriental Jews in Israel today, and are not strictly speaking Sephardic, although they are generally included in that community for purposes of distinction from the Ashkenazi Jews.

ASHREI. Psalm 145, recited twice daily in the morning service and in the afternoon prayer. The Talmud cites Rabbi Eliezer as saying that whoever recites this psalm thrice daily is assured of entering the world to come.

ASYLUM. A person who committed manslaughter or an unpremeditated murder, according to Biblical law, had the right to asylum so as to avoid the vengence of the decedent's relatives. In Bible times there were cities of refuge to which these accidental killers could escape.

ATONEMENT, DAY OF. *See* Yom Kippur.

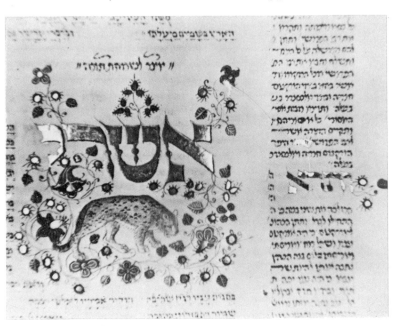

Ashrei from a page in the Machzor manuscript depicting the leopard, the symbol of faith. Italy, c. 1485.

AUTO-DA-FÉ. *See* Inquisition.

AV. 11th month of the Jewish religious year.

AV, 15TH OF. 15th day of the Hebrew month Av, which falls in midsummer. A popular festival in the Second Temple era. According to the Talmud, unmarried girls would all put on white garments and go out to the vineyards, where they would dance, in the hope that eligible bachelors would choose them as future wives. It was also the last day of the year that wood could be brought to the Temple for the wood offering.

AV, 9TH OF. *See* Tisha B'Av.

AVEL (pl. avelim). Mourner. Jewish law provides for periods of mourning by next of kin for their dead. The laws form a whole body of practices, subjecting the mourners to restrictions (e.g., no visiting of places of entertainment), and prescribing recitation of prayers memorializing the decedent. Generally the mourners are immediate blood relatives who, following the funeral, remain at home for a week (in the period of shivah), the men not shaving, seated on low stools, with the mourner's prayer (kaddish) recited thrice daily, and visitors coming to pay their respects and offer comfort in their bereavement. The 30-day period of mourning (called *shloshim*—"thirty") is the most solemn part of the observance, and follows immediately after the funeral. An avel who enters the synagogue for the first time after his loss, at Sabbath eve services, is greeted with a special blessing by all members of the congregation.

AVELEI ZION. (Hebrew for "mourners of Zion.") Groups of Jews who, after the destruction of the Second Temple in the year 70, observed periods of mourning and carried out other ascetic practices, praying for redemption. One group mentioned in the Bible is the *perushim* ("abstainers"), who did not eat meat or drink wine. In the 9th century the Karaites settled in Jerusalem, their leaders declaring that their purpose was to mourn the razed Temple. One noted Jewish traveler of the 12th century, Benjamin of Tudela, reported that he found followers of this practice in Germany and Yemen.

AVERAH (pl. averot). Sin, the opposite of a mitzvah, a good-deed commandment. All sins (as well as mitzvot, pl. of mitzvah) are divided into those against God and those against man. Traditionally, a transgressor in the latter category can attain forgiveness only by requesting and receiving pardon from the person against whom he committed an offense, while sins against God can be nullified by prayer, repentance, and charitable works—in the words of the Yom Kippur liturgy. Jewish teaching assumes that most sins are committed because of human weakness or lack of knowledge, not because of inherent wickedness. If life is imperiled, any *averah* may be carried out, with three exceptions—the shedding of innocent blood, sexual license and idolatry. This explains why even the most devout Jews in Israel did not hesitate to violate the sacred Yom Kippur service to go to their country's defense when the joint Egyptian-Syrian attack of 1973 became known.

AVINU MALKENU. (Hebrew for "our father, our king.") A prayer recited during the ten days of awe (between Rosh Hashanah and Yom Kippur), dating back to the days of Rabbi Akiva. During the course of the centuries additions were made to this moving prayer of supplication, each of whose verses begins with the phrase *"Avinu Malkenu,"* with the total today standing at 44.

AVODAH. (Hebrew for "service.") Refers specifically to the ritual of the Holy Temple and is used today to describe part of the Yom Kippur musaf service. Some Reform temples have incorporated the name as part of their own formal designation.

AVODAH ZARAH. (Hebrew for "idolatry.") One of the Talmudic tracts dealing with idol worship and pagan practices, expounding and elaborating the Biblical prohibitions against heathen customs.

AVOT. (Hebrew for "fathers.") Generally used to refer to the Patriarchs—Abraham, Isaac, and Jacob. The three shared certain basic traits—nobility of character, hospitality, and readiness to help others, the archetypes of ethical conduct taught by Judaism.

AZAZEL. During Temple days, as part of the Yom Kippur service, the High Priest would choose two goats, cast lots, and select one "for the Lord" and drive the other to Azazel—into the wilderness. The latter goat carried with it, symbolically, all the transgressions of the worshipers. The precise meaning of the term is not clear: some define it as a place name and others as a scapegoat. Mystics equated the term with a prototype of Satan. In modern usage the word has become synonymous with a curse.

B

BAAL. Phoenician term for the Lord; loosely used to designate an idol. During the early period of the Israelites' settlement in Canaan, many became worshipers of Baal. In modern Hebrew, the word means both "husband" and "master."

BAAL HABAYIT. (Hebrew for "master.") In colloquial usage, the term (generally pronounced in the Yiddish version, *Baal habayis*) has come to mean an upright, respected person.

BAAL KRIAH. (Hebrew for "master of the reading.") Person who reads from the scroll of the Law in the synagogue as part of the morning service, on Sabbath, holidays, and also on Mondays and Thursdays. The reader is sometimes also called the *Baal koreh*.

BAAL NES. (Hebrew for "master of the miracle.") Although originally this referred to a person to whom something miraculous had occurred, it came to mean a saintly individual who could work miracles, generally a Rabbi who, it was believed, could avert a personal or communal disaster.

BAAL SHEM. (Hebrew for "master of the [divine] name.") Term that came into usage in the Middle Ages, particularly in mystical literature. It denoted someone who used the power of pronouncing God's name to perform miracles. Men who professed to such powers were often called upon to heal the sick or exorcise a dybbuk.

Baal Shem Tov

BAAL SHEM TOV. Israel Ben Eliezer (18th century), the founder of the Hasidic movement. Authentic biographical material is unavailable, but he is believed to have been orphaned as a small child, spending considerable time alone in the woods, meditating in solitude in his Russian village in Podolia. Although he studied constantly, he did not reveal the extent of his learning, and for many years lived the simple life of an unlearned Jew, earning his living as a teacher's assistant and sexton. He later came to be known as a miracle worker, distributing amulets to the sick and comforting those in need.

BAAL TEKIAH. (Hebrew for "master of the blowing.") One who is called upon, during the Rosh Hashanah service, and at the conclusion of the Yom Kippur service, to sound the shofar.

BAAL TEPHILA. (Hebrew for "master of prayer.") One who leads the congregation (or a minyan) in prayer. Contrasted with a cantor or *Hazan,* who does the same, but generally possesses a beautiful voice and is expected to add to the aesthetics of the service. The *Baal Tephila* need only chant the prayers.

BAAL TESHUVA. (Hebrew for "penitent.") One who atones for his sins, literally, a "master of the return." Tradition teaches that a penitent is on a higher spiritual plane than a tzaddik, a righteous person who has never sinned. Some American Jews who have in recent years embraced the strict Orthodox teachings of the Hasidic movement consider themselves penitents, as do some Soviet Jews who have emigrated to Israel where, often for the first time in their lives, they are able to observe Jewish religious laws and customs.

BAHUR. (Hebrew for "chosen one.") The Biblical usage of *bahur* is a young man in his prime, the obverse side of *betulah,* a virgin. Later, and to this day, the term is used to denote a bachelor, especially an unmarried (and presumably eligible for marriage) yeshivah student.

BAHYA, BEN JOSEPH IBN PAKUDA. Late 11th-century Spanish philosopher whose best-known work, *Duties of the Heart,* remains an important ethical guide. He was a judge in a Rabbinic court, and in his philosophy taught the need for diligence in pursuing virtue. He believed that men could understand God through contemplation of creation, and through a moderately ascetic way of life. He also stressed the need for constant self-examination, humility, and striving for a spiritual life that leads to understanding God.

BAR MITZVAH. The occasion on which a boy of 13 is formally ushered into the adult Jewish community, and is expected to assume full religious duties, including responsibility for his own actions—for which his father had been accountable. Generally celebrated by a young man's being called to the Torah reading at Sabbath services, where he is honored by being permitted to chant aloud the Prophetic portion of the week (known as the haftarah). Among Orthodox Jews a bar mitzvah is also expected to deliver himself of a learned discourse on a Talmudic theme. Among most Jews the occasion is celebrated by a festive reception. The bar mitzvah celebration as known today is of late origin, and was not known in

The inauguration of a boy as a member
of the holy house of Israel, 1877.

Biblical days. In addition to bar mitzvah, Reform Jews hold a confirmation service, generally at the age of 16 or 17, at which the youth reiterates his or her attachment to the teachings of Judaism.

BARAITA. (Aramaic for "outside teaching.") The writings of the Tannaim that were not included in the Mishnah, as compiled by Judah ha-Nasi. These include the Tosefta and Halachic Midrashim; some of the latter are scattered in various sections of the Babylonian and Palestinian Talmuds.

BARRENNESS. Since Judaism's 613 mitzvot or precepts begin with the Biblical injunction to "be fruitful and multiply" (Genesis 1:22), the inability to produce offspring has always been considered a great tragedy by Jews. The craving for children, as voiced by Rachel, Sarah, Rebecca, and Hannah in the Bible, indicates the importance attached to children in Jewish teaching. The principal purpose of marriage, as interpreted by the Rabbis who called marriage a duty, was procreation. In Talmudic law a man is required to divorce his wife if she remains barren for ten years. Since the Middle Ages there have been no recorded cases of divorces growing out of barrenness, but the ancient law, in theory at least, remains valid. Among certain communities, notably in the Arab countries, a wife's barrenness is reason enough for the husband to take a second wife. (Polygamy was still in force, as in Biblical times, among the Yemenite Jews in the early 1950s; some of them immigrated to Israel in polygamous marriages.) Polygamy was outlawed in Israel for all Sephardi Jews in 1950. Monogamy is now the religious and civil law of the land.

BARUCH DAYAN HA-EMET. (Hebrew for "Blessed be the true Judge.") Inasmuch as Jews are expected to praise God on both joyous and sorrowful occasions, news of a death is usually greeted by recitation of the blessing, "Blessed art thou, O Lord our God, King of the Universe, the true Judge."

BARUCH HASHEM. (Hebrew for, literally, "Blessed be the name" [of God].) The equivalent phrase in English would be a simple "Thank God"; in Hebrew there is a somewhat stronger religious connotation.

BARUCH HU UVARUCH SHMO. (Hebrew for "Blessed be he and blessed be his name.") The congregation's response, recited in unison, upon hearing the benediction beginning with the phrase "Blessed art thou" (*"Baruch Atah Adoshem"*). At the blessing's conclusion, the congregation responds, "Amen."

BARUCH SHEPETERANI. The opening words of a special blessing recited by the father of a boy about to become bar mitzvah, which expresses thanks to God for "freeing me" from the responsibility for the child (referring to religious accountability only).

BAT MITZVAH. The equivalent of bar mitzvah, only celebrated by girls, generally at the age of 12 or 13, particularly among Conservative and Reform Jews. A very recent innovation, first introduced in the U.S., the bat mitzvah (sometimes called bas mitzvah) is called to the Torah at Friday evening services, where she reads the week's Prophetic portion aloud, and is expected from that point on to assume the responsibilities of a young Jewish woman. Here, too, the religious ceremony is generally followed by a festive reception.

BEARD. Wearing a beard in Biblical times was considered a symbol of manhood; it was carefully trimmed and, in honor of Sabbath and festivals, even anointed. The Biblical prohibition against marring the "edges of your beard" was generally interpreted by the Rabbis as meaning shaving was banned—a prohibition that contemporary Rabbis have gotten around without seeming to ignore the rule itself by permitting use of an electric razor.

BEDIKAH. (Hebrew for "inspection.") Usually used in questions of ritual purity, bedikah is carried out to determine that the knife of a *shochet* is sharp enough (so as not to cause undue pain to an animal about to be slaughtered), or that the animal's lungs show no signs of disease, which would cause the animal to be considered unclean. Witnesses in a civil court are also examined; this is called *bedikat ha-edim*.

BEDIKAT HAMETZ. (Hebrew for "search for leaven.") A ceremonial search carried out on the day before Passover to assure that the home contains no leaven. Today it is a formal ritual in which the head of the household, often holding a symbolic candle, looks for hametz (which his wife has carefully prepared for him in advance), and burns the leaven the next morning (preceding the evening seder), reciting a special blessing. Young children often tag along during the ceremony.

BELLS. Decorations on the scroll of the Law, mounted on the finials and usually made of silver. They usually represent a crown or two towers, and have bells attached. The inspiration for the bells originates with the Biblical description of the High Priest's robe.

BENÇAO (also known as *besam*). The Sephardic equivalent of the Ashkenazi *bentshen*—"grace after meals."

BENE ISRAEL. (Hebrew for "sons of Israel.") Jews of India, principally in the Bombay area. Although their origin is uncertain, they believe they are descended from the ten lost tribes, and wandered into what is today India around the 3d or 4th century. They at first knew little Hebrew and observed only a few of the Jewish holidays and rituals. Some 300 years ago they were discovered by David Rahabi of Cochin, who succeeded in introducing them to all of contemporary Judaism's practices and observances. A large percentage have emigrated to Israel, where they have encountered difficulties with the Israel Rabbinate, which has not fully accepted them as bona fide Jews, primarily because for centuries they did not adhere to Rabbinic teachings dealing with marriage and divorce.

BENEDICTIONS. Since ancient times it has been customary to greet people or refer to them in the framework of a blessing, e.g., *"Ha-Shem yishmer-ahu"* ("May God protect him"); *"Shelitah"*—an acronym for *"Sheyichyeh l'orech yamim tovim amen"* ("May he live long and happily, amen"); *"Zichrono l'vrachah"* ("May his memory be blessed"); *"Alav hashalom"* ("May he rest in peace").

BENEDICTIONS ON TORAH. When called to the

reading of the Torah, one recites: "Blessed art thou, O Lord our God, King of the Universe, who has chosen us from all peoples, and hast given us thy law." After the reading, the blessing concludes: ". . . who has given us the law of truth, and has planted everlasting life in our midst." There are additional blessings for the haftarah portion (read only on Sabbath and holidays), which express faith in the Torah and the Prophets of Israel, and in the fulfillment of the prophecies regarding the redemption of Israel when the Messiah appears.

BERURIAH. Wife of the 2d-century Rabbi Meir, a leading Tanna, she was renowned for her piety and scholarship. The Talmud cites many of her Halachic and Aggadic sayings. Modern Jewish feminists look upon her as one of the first Jewish women in history (since Bible times) to believe in full equality of the sexes.

BET DIN. (Hebrew for "house of judgment.") Jewish court of law where the principles of Halachah are recognized and followed. It can deal with civil, criminal, and religious cases. The appointment of judges and courts dates to Biblical times; in ancient days even the smallest town had a court consisting of three judges, with the highest judicial body, called a Great Bet Din, also known as the Sanhedrin. It consisted of 71 members and had the right to interpret law and establish new legislation. The court's chief was known as Nasi (president), the same term in use today for Israel's president, and an Av Bet Din ("father of the court"). Jewish courts continued through history, and in Spain were even empowered to adjudicate criminal cases. Today most such courts deal only with religious questions; in Israel they also deal with matters of personal status.

BET HAMIKDASH. Holy Temple. The First Temple was built on Mount Moriah in Jerusalem by Solomon, and was referred to as the House of the Lord. It was destroyed by Nebuchadnezzar in 587 B.C.E. and was rebuilt some 50 years later, thanks to an edict of Cyrus. The Second Temple was destroyed by Titus in 70 C.E. on the ninth day of the Hebrew month Av, which has remained a day of fasting and mourning. The Temple area is now the Mosque of Omar, erected in 700. Only the famed Western Wall still stands.

BET HAYYIM. (Hebrew for "house of life.") Euphemism for a cemetery. Also called Bet Olam ("the eternal home").

BET MIDRASH. (Hebrew for "house of learning.") During Talmudic days the term was synonymous with academy or yeshivah. In the Middle Ages the Bet Midrash usually adjoined the Bet Knesset (synagogue). In central Europe it was sometimes called the *klaus* or *kloiz,* akin to the Latin term for "cloister." Both popular general study and advanced higher learning were carried out in the Bet Midrash. Students were permitted to spend the night in the Bet Midrash (but not in a synagogue).

BETROTHAL. The concept of an engagement before marriage is well established in Jewish tradition. The terms of a betrothal agreement are called *tenaim* (Hebrew for "conditions").

BETWEEN THE STRAITS. The 21 days (also known as the Three Weeks) between the 17th of Tammuz and the 9th of Av, when many disasters befell the Jewish people, e.g., both Temples were destroyed in this period. The observant do not hold dances and festivities during these three weeks; some do not eat meat or drink wine, except on the Sabbath, and some do not allow the hair to be cut—all as a sign of mourning.

BIBLE. The Hebrew acronym for the Bible is Tanakh, for Torah (the Law, also called the Pentateuch, or Five Books of Moses, consisting of Genesis, Exodus, Leviticus, Numbers, and Deuteronomy), Neviim (Prophets, including Isaiah, Jeremiah, and Ezekiel), and Ketuvim (Holy Writings, also called Hagiographa, including Psalms, Proverbs, Esther, Ruth, Chronicles, and other volumes.) Among non-Jews the Bible is referred to as the Old Testament, to distinguish it from the Christian New Testament. Because of the Bible, Jews have been known for centuries as the People of the Book.

BIBLE, LOST BOOKS OF THE. A number of works

are referred to in Holy Scriptures, but these have been lost. They include the Book of the Wars of the Lord, the Book of Jashar, Words of Samuel the Seer, Words of Nathan the Prophet, and the Chronicles of King David.

BIBLE EXEGESIS. Interpretation of the Bible has been going on for thousands of years. It is today a scientific discipline, aided by linguistics, history, and archaeology. The first such interpreter is considered to be Ezra, who saw the Torah as the law, and that it in turn required expounding and elaboration in the light of changing conditions.

BIKKUR CHOLIM. *See* Sick, Visits to the. (Also known colloquially as *mevaker cholim zein.*)

BIRKAT HAZIMUN. (Hebrew for "benediction of invitation.") An invitation to join in the grace after meals, when three or more adult males are present at the table. The leader says, "My friends, let us bless," to which the others respond, "May the name of the Lord be blessed forever."

BIRTH CONTROL. The sin of a man "spilling his seed on the ground" while living with his wife is considered punishable by death in the Bible. Some Reform Rabbis condone birth control, but most Orthodox Rabbis condemn it, except for serious health reasons. Preference among the permissible methods goes to oral contraceptives—there is a Talmudic reference to a "cup of sterility" drunk by the wife.

BISHOP OF THE JEWS. In medieval England, a Kohen was so designated, while in Germany the term was sometimes used to refer to a Rabbi.

BLASPHEMY. The Bible stipulates that anyone who reviles God is punishable by stoning, but the Talmud restricted capital punishment to those who reviled the Tetragrammaton. Since Jewish courts no longer have the power to order capital punishment, blasphemy has usually been punished by excommunication.

BLESSING OF CHILDREN. There are many Biblical precedents for the blessing of children by parents but the practice of a formal ritual (usually on the eve of

Sabbath) is a recent innovation. The customary phrase for a boy is "God make thee as Ephraim and Manasseh"; for a girl, "God make thee as Sarah, Rebecca, Rachel, and Leah." The parent places both hands on the child's head while intoning the benediction.

BLESSING OVER BREAD. Popular benediction offered at the beginning of a meal. It absolves the diner from the necessity of reciting separate blessings for each part of the meal. The blessing (frequently heard also at public Jewish meals) concludes with the words "Who brings forth bread from the earth . . . *hamotzi lechem min haaretz.*"

BLOOD. Biblical law forbids the consumption of blood of animals, since this is tantamount to eating the living animal. The system of kashering, i.e., soaking the meat in water, salting, and rinsing, was instituted to remove the last traces of blood from a ritually slaughtered animal. Since liver is regarded as containing so much blood, it must be grilled on an open fire before consumption.

BLOOD LIBEL. An accusation that sprang up in the Middle Ages, in the 19th century, and again during the Nazi era, that Jews used the blood of a Christian child for religious rites, especially for baking matzah for Passover. The allegation, which is of course groundless, has been formally and repeatedly denounced by a number of Popes.

BODEK. (Hebrew for "examiner.") Official who examines a slaughtered animal to determine if it is ritually pure and therefore edible. The inspection is usually done by the slaughterer himself; hence he is called a *shohet u'vodek*—a ritual slaughterer and examiner.

BOOK. Jewish tradition has always displayed great reverence for books. A sacred book that slips to the ground is immediately picked up and kissed. Worn out and unusable holy books are never thrown away but stored in the synagogue's genizah (storeroom). The scroll of the Law is known in Hebrew as the *Sefer Torah* ("the book of the Law"). Acquiring books and

הברת
נעילנרית אברהם

Chair of Elijah, used at circumcisions.
Italy, 18th century.

lending them to needy students was considered a religious good deed. In our day Jews wishing to honor or memorialize someone will give prayer books, Bibles, or books of Jewish content to their synagogue, synagogue library, or religious school.

BOOK OF LIFE. Tradition holds that Jews will be inscribed in the heavenly Book of Life on Rosh Hashanah, and that the inscription will be sealed ten days later, on Yom Kippur. Hence, customary greetings on the Jewish New Year express the hope that "you will be inscribed for a good life" in the coming year.

BRACHAH. Blessing, for food, for holidays, on being called to the Torah, for use under the wedding canopy, after an escape from potential disaster, etc. A special blessing is often recited in the synagogue on Sabbath morning for members of the congregation (or their friends and relatives) who are seriously ill.

BRIBERY. The Bible clearly forbids any bribes, and holds that both the giver and the taker are culpable, but especially directs its prohibition against a judge whose objectivity would be destroyed by acceptance of a bribe. To keep judges from being tempted by bribes it became the practice of the community as a whole to pay their salaries.

BRINGING IN THE BRIDE. (*Hachnasat kalah* in Hebrew.) Custom allowing discreet aid to a poor girl about to be married, by providing her with the necessary clothes and household utensils and furniture so as not to enter into a marriage penniless. Special societies of women were formed in many communities to help provide for the bride. The custom, in modified form, is still in force in Israel, where a disproportionately large number of young women—victims of the Holocaust—were without parents to usher them into married life.

BRIT MILAH. Circumcision. Sometimes called, in the Yiddish version, a *bris*. An operation removing part or all of the foreskin covering the glans penis. It is generally carried out on the eighth day after birth, and expresses the child's entering into a covenant with God, in the tradition of Abraham's covenant with God described in the Bible. The operation is usually performed by a mohel; the godfather who holds the child on his lap is called the sandak, and the chair he is seated on is called the chair of Elijah. After the circumcision a festive meal is offered to the invited guests.

BUBER, MARTIN. Religious philosopher (1878–1965) whose thought moved from mysticism to existentialism. With Franz Rosenzweig he translated the Bible into German (he was born in Germany), and interpreted Hasidism to the modern world. Christian theologians have been greatly influenced by his Biblical interpretation, which was highly personal, i.e., as between man and God.

Martin Buber

BURGLARY. According ,to Bible law a thief found breaking into a home may be killed by the owner on the assumption that the perpetrator knows every man will do whatever is necessary to defend his home, and the burglar is therefore prepared to kill the owner, if need be. The owner is permitted to anticipate the burglar and kill in self-defense—but not during daylight hours, when it is assumed the burglar has broken in solely to steal; in such a case, the householder would be guilty of a capital crime.

BURIAL. Proper burial, even for a convicted criminal, is a strong Jewish tradition. Communal groups known as *Hevrah Kadisha* look after the burial needs of the Jewish dead, although in most western societies the responsibility has been taken over by commercial funeral chapels. Jewish law provides that burial must take place as soon after death as possible. The body is first bathed and wrapped in a plain shroud and placed in a coffin; in Israel and in eastern countries a coffin is not used. The body is brought to a cemetery and following a brief ceremony is lowered into the ground, with those in attendance helping to fill in the grave and the next of kin reciting the kaddish prayer. Cremation is forbidden by Jewish law, but some Reform Jews practice it.

BURNT OFFERING. A sacrifice, in Bible times, in which the entire animal was consumed by fire, with nothing returned to the sacrificer or priest except the skin. This type of sacrifice was meant to atone for the sin of pride.

CALENDAR. The Jewish calendar, although based on a complicated set of rules, is so accurate that the requirement that Yom Kippur, for example, never fall on Friday or Hoshanah Rabba on Saturday is met with ease. Broadly speaking, the months are based on the moon and the years on the sun. Since the lunar year is only 354 days, an extra month (Adar II) is added seven times during a 19-year solar period. There are 12 months in an ordinary year and 13 in a leap year; each month consists of either 29 or 30 days. This explains why widely observed holidays like Rosh Hashanah may fall one year at the beginning of September, and another year at the end.

CANDLE, MOURNING. During the week of mourning (shivah) following the death of a close relative, a mourning candle burns in the home of the mourner. A candle is also kindled on the anniversary of the death (yahrzeit), when the kaddish prayer is recited in the synagogue. A similar yahrzeit candle is lit at home on the eve of Yom Kippur for all those who are mourned during that most solemn of days.

CANDLES, LIGHTING OF. Traditionally, the mistress of the house kindles candles on the eve of Sabbath or holidays, reciting an appropriate blessing to symbolize bringing a festive atmosphere into the home. (All Jewish holidays, festivals, and the Sabbath begin on the evening preceding the day itself.) At least two candles are lit; in some households the number is increased, sometimes to parallel the number of members of the family. When reciting the blessing, the woman of the house covers her head with a kerchief, holds her hands before her eyes, recites the blessing silently, and then exclaims "Good Sabbath" or "happy holiday" (whichever is appropriate). If there are others present they reply in kind. Among the very Orthodox, very young girls are encouraged to light candles, even as early as age 3.

CANTILLATION. *See* Accents.

CANTOR. A *hazzan*, or the leader of congregational prayer, also known as a *shliach tzibur* (the public's representative) since he is delegated by the congregation to lead them in prayers to the Almighty. A cantor is expected not only to have a pleasing voice but to be a pious Jew, worthy of the signal honor accorded him. In Hasidic services the role of the cantor is played down with the emphasis on equal, collective prayer by all worshipers; in Reform services the cantor's role is enhanced, and his singing is often accompanied by an organist.

CAPITAL PUNISHMENT. Biblical law called for the

death sentence for a wide variety of crimes, but implementation of the sentence was rare. Rabbinic interpretation called for two witnesses to be present at the crime, and that the violator be given ample warning prior to committing his crime—conditions which, obviously, could not be met easily. Talmudic Rabbis said that a court that sentenced even one man to the death penalty during a 70-year period was bloodthirsty. A capital case may be tried by a Bet Din of no fewer than 23 judges. In modern Israel, capital punishment has been abolished except in cases of genocide or wartime treason.

CAPTIVES. The redemption of Jews held in captivity is considered one of the most important Jewish religious duties, taking precedence even over charity. Delay in ransoming captives, according to Maimonides, was equal to spilling blood. Captives include Jews taken by the enemy as a result of warfare, or Jews persecuted by oppressive regimes, or Jewish children kidnapped by non-Jewish neighbors who then sought to hide the captives' true origins. The problem of redeeming captives reached a high point in the Middle Ages; after the expulsion from Spain in 1492 many Jews were sold into slavery. A famous case had occurred in the 13th century when the Emperor Rudolf threw Rabbi Meir of Rothenburg into prison, and the latter forbade his congregants to redeem him for fear that this would lead to widespread seizures of other Rabbis for the sake of exorbitant ransoms.

CARCASS. (*Nevelah* in Hebrew.) Body of an animal that has died other than by ritual slaughter. It may not be eaten but it may be given or sold to a non-Jew.

CASTING LOTS. Ancient practice, used not only by Haman in deciding on what day to launch an attack on the Jews in the Persian kingdom, but also in the division of ancient Israel among the 12 tribes. Jewish law holds that casting lots does not constitute legal evidence.

CASTRATION. Among all the ancient peoples, only the Hebrews forbade the emasculation of men and animals. The prohibition was later extended by the Talmud to impotent men.

CATACOMBS. Burial in Biblical times took place in subterranean caves, with room made for the resting places of the corpses. The practice was carried out in Rome among the Jewish slaves brought there after the destruction of the Second Temple, and was adopted by the Christians. Jewish symbols, including the menorah, *lulav*, and *etrog*, have often been found in the catacombs.

CELIBACY. The practice was strongly frowned on; even the ascetic Nazirites and priests were not expected to follow the custom (which was probably practiced among the Essenes, however). Indeed, Rabbinic laws specify that religious leaders must be married, the occasional exception being the scholar who is totally absorbed in religious studies.

CEMETERY. Jewish law provides for a hallowed plot of ground for burial purposes, where any activity such as eating or drinking, which could be regarded as disrespectful of the dead, is forbidden. Many cemeteries contain a building for the performing of burial rites, such as taharah (the washing of the corpse before enshrouding). Suicides, apostates, and people known to have been evil during their lifetimes are generally buried near the cemetery walls, away from the main graves. A suicide of unsound mind, however, may be buried in the normal way, and this is usually done today. The graves of the deceased are visited on the anniversary of the death and before the High Holy Days.

CENSUS. Jewish tradition frowns upon a direct census, reflecting a widely held belief that such an enumeration could lead to tragedy. Thus, to determine if there is a minyan of ten males present (to allow for a full-fledged service), the stratagem is used of having those present recite jointly a Biblical phrase containing ten words.

CENTRAL CONFERENCE OF AMERICAN RABBIS. American-Canadian organization of Reform Rabbis, founded in 1889. With a membership close to 1000, the conference has published Reform-oriented prayer books, Haggadahs, and a manual for ceremonial occasions. In the early 20th century the group was either non- or anti-Zionist, but reversed itself in the 1930s; a gradual return to the use of more Hebrew and more traditional ritual in the service has been noted in recent years.

CHAI. The numerical equivalent of the two Hebrew letters chet and yod spells the Hebrew word for "life." Donors to charitable causes often give "chai" dollars (or twice or other multiples of chai) when announcing their contributions. In recent years both men and women may be seen wearing a necklace on which the word hangs—as a good-luck charm, and sometimes a display of Jewish identity.

CHANGE OF NAME. God's changing the names of Abraham (from Abram), Sarah (from Sarai), and Israel (from Jacob) is precedent for a person's changing his name in order to invest it with new significance or fortune. A dangerously sick person's name is often changed (in the case of a male to Chayim, "life") —according to tradition, to mislead the angel of death.

CHAPLAINS. The appointment of religious chaplains attached to the military is a fairly recent innovation. The first American Jewish chaplain was appointed during the Civil War. The U.S. armed forces had, during World War II, more than 300 Jewish chaplains in active service. In the present-day Israel Defense Forces there is a chaplain attached to each brigade.

CHARITY. (*Tzedakah* in Hebrew.) The Hebrew word is related to *tzedek* ("justice"), since the giving of material help to the needy has always been a cardinal Jewish principle. In a famous dictum, Maimonides tabulated eight degrees of charity—the highest form of which was to help the needy person to help himself out of his impoverished circumstances. Jewish homes often have a pushka, a small container, into which coins are dropped, often just before the kindling of Sabbath eve candles. When full, the container is emptied and the contents sent off to a deserving charity. Religious schoolchildren are encouraged from an early age to develop the habit of regular donations to worthy causes.

CHERUB. The Bible relates the story of the cherubim

(pl.) who stood at the Garden of Eden when Adam and Eve were driven out after committing the sin of eating of the tree of knowledge. They are described in Ezekiel as winged four-faced creatures; likenesses of the cherubim were placed in front of the ark in the First Temple, their wings serving as protection. Most commentators believe they are akin to prevalent Egyptian myths of ancient times, although the Midrash says they are among the highest class of angels.

CHIEF RABBINATE. In the Middle Ages local Chief Rabbis were often communal tax collectors, or acted as liaisons between the Jewish community and the authorities. There are Chief Rabbis in England, Israel, France, Ireland, and a few other countries (not in the U.S.); in Israel, the title is divided between the Ashkenazi and Sephardi Chief Rabbis. There is a general feeling that since any qualified Rabbi has the authority to determine points of religious law, there is need for one overall Rabbinic Supervisor, at least until such time as a new Sanhedrin may be reconvened. In the U.S., although there are no Chief Rabbis per se, there are, especially among the Orthodox, a few distinguished Rabbinic scholars who may be considered the leading Rabbis of the day.

CHILDBIRTH. Jewish tradition does not regard the pain of childbirth as obligatory, and permits women in labor to receive whatever medical aid will help them overcome the suffering of giving birth. Biblical law stipulates that a woman who has given birth to a boy is considered ritually impure for 33 days, and if the child is a girl, 66 days. A male child born by cesarean section is not considered a firstborn. If a woman has a miscarriage of a boy, her next child, if a boy, is not considered firstborn.

CHOIR. The use of a choir, as distinct from congregational singing, is of very recent vintage. Conservative and Reform synagogues generally feature choirs during the service, especially on holidays. Orthodox congregations prefer to concentrate on congregational singing at services.

CHOLENT. Sabbath dish popular among Ashkenazic Jews, especially in eastern Europe. Since cooking on the Sabbath was not allowed, the cholent (a meat, potatoes, and bean mixture) was prepared on Friday and allowed to keep warm all through Friday night until the midday Sabbath meal that followed morning services.

CHOSEN PEOPLE. Deeply rooted Jewish concept that the Jewish people were chosen, in a special relationship to God, to relate his message to mankind. Thus it is interpreted by Jewish thinkers as a mission, rather than an attempt to describe Jews as superior or unique. The idea is closely linked to the tradition that Jews are a holy people. Converts to Judaism are considered to be equal to born Jews in this concept of chosenness. Nevertheless, among Reform and Reconstructionist Jews the concept has been deleted from the liturgy.

CIRCUMCISION. *See* Brit Milah.

CITY OF REFUGE. In Biblical times a person who had committed unpremeditated murder could flee to one of six cities of refuge to escape the vengeance of next of kin. Roads leading to these towns had to be clearly marked, to ensure the safe arrival of killers seeking haven.

CLEAN AND UNCLEAN ANIMALS. Jewish dietary

Animals forbidden as food.

laws divide animals that may be eaten into clean and unclean. Noah took seven pairs of clean animals into the ark but only two pairs of the unclean. Permissible animals that may be eaten (four-legged) are those that have cloven hooves and chew their cud. Clean fishes are those with both scales and fins. Shellfish are not permissible. Most fowl may be eaten, with about a score classed as unclean.

CLEANLINESS. Biblical and Rabbinic literature emphasizes the need for personal hygiene. Maimonides, himself a scholar-philosopher and physician, said that one goal of the Bible was to effect an appearance of outward cleanliness which would reflect inner purity. Ritual cleanliness, such as laws with regard to the mikveh, is considered separate and apart from the need for individual attention to sanitary habits.

CODES OF JEWISH LAW. Although the Talmud is the basis of Jewish law today, and it in turn is based on the Bible, it requires an expert to ascertain clear-cut rules and decrees. The codes are a body of literature that interprets and expounds on possibilities of law, and is primarily for the scholar rather than for the judge seeking specific rulings or precedents. A great number of codes of law have been developed during the past centuries, the major one being the *Mishneh Torah* of Maimonides, and the *Shulchan Aruch* of Joseph Karo, completed in the 16th century. The latter is most often regarded as the basis of contemporary Jewish religious law.

COMFORTING THE BEREAVED. Providing solace to the mourner is an ancient Jewish tradition. It is customary today to visit the bereaved person while he is observing the mourning period (shivah), and to say to him, "May the Almighty comfort you together with those who mourn for Zion and Jerusalem." The same greeting is extended to the mourner by the congregation when he enters the synagogue on Friday evening, after the funeral.

COMMENTARY. The tradition of commenting on and interpreting Scriptures is ancient, dating to Ezra the Scribe. Two main schools of commentary have always been evident: *p'shat* (simple, commonsensical) and *d'rash* (investigative, or deliberative). The latter calls for a more imaginative analyst of the textual material, who can read between the lines and make the laws and precepts relevant to the tenor and needs of the time. The Talmud, including the Halachah (law) and Haggadah (homily) sections, is a huge interpretation and exposition of Bible teachings. However, if a simple, literal explanation (p'shat) is acceptable, it is considered preferable. The foremost founder of the *p'shat* school of commentary was Rabbi Saadyah Gaon. Probably the most popular and all-encompassing commentator is Rashi, who lived in France in the 11th century, and whose work is still studied by all Bible students.

COMPASSION. A trait that marks the Jewish people, and one which led the Rabbis of old to say that the Jews are "compassionate children of compassionate fathers." God, in Jewish tradition, is described as the Compassionate One—inspiring mere mortals to emulate this divine characteristic. In law, the Talmud warns that "compassion must figure in the handing down of legal judgments."

CONDUCT (*Derech eretz* in Hebrew.) Both the Bible and post-Biblical literature stress the importance of good conduct, including manners, etiquette, dignified behavior, hospitality, teacher-student relations, and other social contacts. "*Derech eretz* not only precedes Torah," the Rabbis taught, "but without *derech eretz* there is no Torah."

CONFESSION. (*Vidui* in Hebrew.) One of the three essential ingredients of true repentance, the other two being regret and determination not to repeat the wrongdoing. Confession, in Jewish thought, is made directly to God, either privately or as part of the congregational confessional on Yom Kippur. Confession of past sins on one's deathbed is encouraged in theory, but in modern times this usually remains academic, since attending physicians do not like to upset a dying patient by telling him it is time for his *vidui*.

CONGRATULATIONS. "*Mazal tov!*" ("Good luck!") is a well-known expression of congratulations, offered on many different occasions. Others include the phrase offered to one who has just been honored by being called to the reading of the Torah in the synagogue, *"Yiyasher koch'cha"* ("May God increase your strength")—in daily usage, the phrase often comes out as *"Yasher koach." "L'chayim"* ("to life") is a popular toast, while the wish that a birthday celebrant live to be 120 reminds one of the age at which Moses died.

CONSERVATIVE JUDAISM. American-inspired religious movement that originated in the 20th century, with some ties to earlier groups in Europe. The movement seeks to conserve the traditions of Judaism while being enlightened about the need for reasonable changes in ritual and observances. It differs basically from Reform, which abandoned the traditional Halachah, although Conservative thinking is ready to amend or modify Halachah—a step that the Orthodox wing of Judaism refuses to even consider. Unlike the Reform and certain sections of the Orthodox communities, Conservative Judaism was pro-Zionist from its inception, seeing in a renascent Israel a spiritual center for Jews throughout the world. The Rabbinic arm of the movement, the Rabbinic Assembly, recognizes both majority and minority viewpoints; thus in some synagogues women may be called to the Torah or counted in a minyan, while in others they may not.

CONSISTORY. Governing body of a Jewish district, first established by Napoleon in 1808, and still in force in France and Belgium. Included in the governing body are clerical and lay leaders. In France there is a central consistory in Paris made up of three Grand Rabbis and two laymen, who are responsible for the office of the Chief Rabbinate and the Rabbinic seminary in France.

CONVERSION, FORCED. Compulsory conversion to Christianity and Islam, respectively, occurred as early as the 4th century in the Roman Empire. At the time of the Crusades many Jewish communities, particularly those living in and around the Rhineland, were ordered to convert or be put to death; many Jews preferred death, the most famous case being that of the Jewish community in York, in the 12th century, where every member committed self-immolation.

After the worst of these waves of persecution had spent themselves, the Jews who had been living as Christians applied for permission to return to the Jewish fold, great Rabbinic leaders of the day urged that they be accepted back, and treated with discretion, with no questions asked about their previous experience. The Rabbis ordered, also, that Jews who accepted the dominant faith outwardly but continued to practice Judaism secretly be treated as full Jews rather than as apostates. Similar forced conversions were launched in the Muslim world in the 12th century. The largest numbers of forced converts were in Spain, where the practitioners of secret Judaism (known as Marranos) were numerous.

COSTUME. Biblical law prohibits the wearing of clothing of members of the opposite sex, and against wearing shatnez, cloth derived from mixing wool and linen. Jews are also to put fringes (tzitzit) on the four corners of their garments. The first ban has been interpreted to refer primarily to men who don women's garments for immoral purposes. In the Talmudic period, wearing distinctive "Jewish" clothes became popular as a weapon against possible assimilation of the Jews by the dominant community. Hasidim today still wear a mode of clothing once popular among Polish noblemen, including a fur-trimmed hat (shtreiml) and a long, usually black caftan.

COVENANT. (Brit in Hebrew.) God's covenant with Abraham is a basic prerequisite to understanding the development of the Jewish religion. The original covenant was considered to have been renewed when the Israelites at Mount Sinai accepted the "two tablets of the covenant," i.e., the Ten Commandments and, by extension, the Torah. Circumcision (brit milah) is the visible manifestation of the continuing validity of the covenant.

COVERING THE HEAD. Covering of the head, a strong feature of Orthodox observance (for males), both at prayer and in everyday activity, is not mentioned in the Bible. It began in antiquity as a custom showing reverence for God and acknowledging his omnipresence. The High Priest in Bible times was instructed to wear a miter but otherwise, apparently, bareheadedness was the custom of the time. A 13th-century Rabbi, indicating that the practice was then not universally in vogue, complained of young boys studying the Torah with their heads uncovered. In most Reform temples the prayers are recited by men with their heads uncovered; in Conservative synagogues, men cover their heads.

CROWN OF LAW. (*Keter Torah* in Hebrew.) One of the decorations of the scroll of the Law, usually made of gold or silver in the shape of a large crown, with two sockets into which are inserted the tops of the rollers to which is fastened the handwritten Torah. The term also denotes a mark of learning.

CUP OF BENEDICTION. (*Kos shel brachah* in Hebrew.) The drinking of wine on joyous occasions, such as a circumcision or wedding, is an important Jewish ritual, despite the traditional Jewish opposition to all forms of drunkenness. The kiddush, recited for wine on the eves of Sabbath and holidays, as well as at the Passover service seder, is an integral part of Jewish tradition.

Kiddush cups. Left: Frankfurt, early 18th century.
Center: Nuremberg, 1761. Right: Russia, 19th century.

CUSTOM. (*Minhag* in Hebrew.) As interpreted by the Rabbis, a minhag is a religious custom dating to post-Biblical days that has become hallowed by the course of time. There are religious customs purely local in character, while even more universally practiced religious customs are thought to be less binding than formal religious law. An example is the observance (outside Israel) of additional days for certain holidays, e.g., Passover, Shavouth, Sukkoth—customs that are now virtually part and parcel of the tradition even though the original reasons for their institution may no longer be valid.

D

DAHVEN. Yiddish word whose origins are unknown (although the word may be related to the English "divine"), meaning "to pray." Sephardic Jews do not use the word. A worshiper may be said to be *dahven-ing* with *kavanah*—utter devotion.

DANCE. As a means of expressing religious joy and personal happiness, dance has always been a feature of Jewish life. When the Israelites crossed safely to the other side of the Red Sea, Moses' sister Miriam led the women in a dance; King David leaped and danced with joy when the holy ark arrived safely in Jerusalem, while in Talmudic times Rabbis joined the celebrants in dance at the wedding of a newly married couple, always careful to avoid mixed dancing, i.e., men and women danced separately. The modern Hasidim place great store on the dance as a mode of expressing their religious ecstasy. On Simhat Torah, at the conclusion of the Sukkoth holiday, dancing with the scrolls of the Law is a traditional part of the synagogue service. A popular concession among the Orthodox to the prohibition against mixed dancing is the handkerchief dance, where a married couple may hold separate ends of a handkerchief as they cavort on the floor, never actually touching each other.

DANGER. Rabbinic teaching explained two Biblical commandments about avoiding danger as a duty to pursue a moderate and safe·course in all walks of life. Among the prohibitions listed in the Talmud are those forbidding entry into a ruined building, drinking contaminated water, and ignoring dietary precautions. The concept of *pikuach nefesh*—the requirement that one may go to any length to save a human life—is a strongly entrenched basis of Judaism, and nullifies all other conflicting laws with the exception of the three sins of idolatry, immorality, and shedding of innocent blood. Thus a sick person who insists on fasting on Yom Kippur, despite his physician's warnings, is considered as having violated observance of the day.

DARSHAN. (Hebrew for "one who expounds.") A public preacher in the synagogue or academy who usually intermixed religious law with homily in his expositions. The custom of such public teaching and preaching dates to Talmudic times when people would come to listen to the Darshan, in addition to participating in the service. In the Middle Ages and somewhat later, a Darshan was often invited to deliver himself of a learned and stimulating talk at wedding receptions.

DAY OF ATONEMENT. *See* Yom Kippur.

DAY OF JUDGMENT. Traditionally, at the end of days, or *acharit hayamim*, the final judgment of mankind will be made by God, or by one of his appointed. The prophets of old warned that at that time all evildoers, including those among the Jews, would be punished for their sins.

DAYS OF AWE. (*Yamin noraim* in Hebrew.) The ten days of penitence, from the 1st day of Tishri (Rosh Hashanah) through the 10th (Yom Kippur), traditionally a time for self-examination and resolve to repent, when the fear of divine judgment hovers above.

DAYYAN. A judge in a Rabbinic court.

DAYYENU. Popular section of the Passover seder service, in which all participants sing together of God's bounty to the Jewish people. May date back to the 6th century.

DEAD, ACCOMPANYING OF. (*Halvayat hamet* in

Hebrew.) It is considered a great mitzvah to join a funeral cortege to the cemetery. Traditionally, if one sees a strange cortege en route to the cemetery, he should accompany it at least a short distance, as a sign of respect for the deceased.

Scroll from the Qumrân Cave I, the Great Isaiah Scroll.

DEAD SEA SCROLLS. Ancient scrolls discovered in 1947 in caves near the Dead Sea, including complete copies and fragments of books of the Bible, making these the oldest known manuscripts of the Old Testament. Some scrolls were hitherto unknown works of a sect of the Second Temple period who lived in the Dead Sea vicinity, and whose views of life seem close to those of the ascetic Essenes. The scrolls are in square Hebrew script, Aramaic, and ancient Hebrew script. One of the conclusions drawn from the scrolls concerned the origins of Christianity, which appeared to be more firmly rooted in ancient Judaism than had previously been known.

DEAF, IMBECILE, AND MINOR. Because they were considered to be wanting in understanding, deaf-and-dumb persons, imbeciles, and minors were ruled by the Talmud to have no legal responsibilities. They were exempted from punishment if they caused injury, but those causing them injury were punishable. The Rabbis made a distinction between one who is both deaf and mute and one who suffers from only one of these afflictions.

DEATH, ANNIVERSARY OF. (*Yahrzeit* in Yiddish.) The anniversary, according to the Hebrew date, of the death of a close relative. It is customary to light a special 24-hour candle on this date and to recite kaddish at the three daily services corresponding to the anniversary. Many people also memorialize loved ones by contributing to charity on the same day.

DECALOGUE. The Greek term for the Ten Commandments (literally, the "ten words") given by God to Moses on Mount Sinai. Jewish thought holds that the Ten Commandments form the sum and substance of Judaism, and that all 613 commandments are found, directly or obliquely, in the Decalogue. The Ten Commandments are listed twice in the Bible. When they are read aloud at synagogue services the congregation rises—symbolic of the time when the Israelites stood at the foot of Mount Sinai while Moses, high up on the mountain, received the commandments from God.

DEDICATION. Formal consecration of a plot for use as a cemetery or a building for religious purposes. It is accompanied by a Bible-inspired ritual. Nowadays the dedication ceremony for a new synagogue building includes affixing the mezuzah to the doorpost and walking around the building while holding the scrolls of the Law. An individual's home may also be considered dedicated after a mezuzah has been fastened to the doorpost, with recitation of the appropriate benediction.

DEFERMENT. When a fast day occurs on the Sabbath it is customary to move the fast to the preceding Thursday or the following Sunday.

DELAY OF PRAYER. (*Ikuv hat'filah* in Hebrew.) A congregant had the right to interrupt the service—generally during the reading of the Torah, on Sabbaths and holidays—if there was an urgent communal affair to be settled, or if he had a grievance against the community. Rabbi Gershom, a 10th-century authority, ruled that a congregant could delay the service if he had asked someone to a court hearing and the latter refused to appear.

DEMONOLOGY. Judaism has little to say about the existence of supernatural beings capable of causing harm to people, but accentuates the omnipotence of God as being able to offset any such possible deeds. Among the people themselves, through history, there was some belief in and fear of demonic spirits. Tales of demons are found in the Aggadah and in popular folklore. The kabbalists in particular voiced belief in an unending battle between demon-inspired evil and the quest for holiness.

DENUNCIATION. One of the most heinous crimes known in the Jewish community, particularly in the Middle Ages, was that of the *malshin* or *moser*, the informer who endangered the interests of the community. Such people could be sentenced to death for their deeds.

DESTROY, THOU SHALT NOT. (*Bal tashchit* in Hebrew.) Wanton destruction of anything that someone else might enjoy is forbidden. Maimonides said that "this is a warning against the uprooting of fruit-bearing trees during the siege of a city so as to harass its inhabitants." The ban includes the senseless destruction of clothes, utensils, or anything that may be of value to another.

DEVEKUT. (Hebrew for "cleavage.") Concept, defined in the Talmud, of a person's seeking to come close to God by imitating his attributes of mercy and kindness. Mystics of old and Hasidim today seek to establish such a communion with God through meditation as well as the performance of good deeds.

DEVOTIONAL LITERATURE. Religious works outside the Bible, Talmud, and prayer book that have as their principal aim an increase of piety and devotion rather than of learning and understanding. Most of these forms of literature are found in Yiddish or Ladino, since they were read largely by the unlettered people. One of the leading examples, read mainly by women, was the Yiddish *Tze'enah U'reenah.*

DEW AND RAIN. Special prayer added to the amidah during the winter months. It is suspended after the special prayer for dew is intoned on Passover.

DIASPORA. The Greek word for "dispersion" refers to those countries, collectively, where Jews outside Israel reside. The Hebrew equivalent (*galut*) implies a forced exile, while Diaspora may be a voluntary self-exile from the land of Israel. Historically, the term indicated the consequences of military defeat and the exile from Israel that followed; religiously, exile was regarded as punishment for the people's sins—and the daily prayers for restoration of the Jewish homeland reflected the people's supplication for forgiveness and a new chance.

DIETARY LAWS. Most dietary laws apply to animal foods. Exceptions include a ban on eating the fruit of a tree in the first three years after it is planted, eating produce before a tithe has been set aside, among the Orthodox, drinking wine prepared or touched by a non-Jew, and sowing mixed seeds in the same field. (The latter prohibition is applicable only in Israel.) The dietary laws aim to inculcate in the diner a sense of holiness at all times, including the daily consumption of food. Tradition holds that in a Messianic period people will desist from eating meat and will subsist on fruits and vegetables, elevating them to a new level of spiritual grandeur. Today meat and milk dishes may not be eaten together; a suitable interval must follow after a meat meal before dairy dishes may be eaten. The dietary laws are extensive; because of changing conditions, Rabbis today are often asked to rule on new problems dealing with food, which arise with surprising frequency. The word "kosher" (pure) indicates that a given food is acceptable. The concept of dietary laws is classed under the laws of *kashrut.* Reform Jews do not observe these laws. Many Conservative Jews observe dietary laws at home but not outside. (*See also* Clean and Unclean Animals.)

DIN. Religious law, or legal decision. Yom Kippur is referred to as Yom ha-Din, the day of judgment.

DIN TORAH. Legal hearing that is held in accordance with the rules of Haláchah.

DISPENSATION. (*Heter* in Hebrew.) Permission by a qualified Rabbinic authority, acting in accordance with Halachah precedents, to relax a given law, observance of which would create undue hardship. Broadly interpreted, such dispensations may be granted in cases of laws originating in Rabbinic commentary or those that are grounded in accepted custom, but not laws stipulated in the Bible.

DISPUTATIONS. Public debates by adherents of different religious persuasions, recorded as early as the days of Josephus, carried out by early Roman philosophers and Jewish religious leaders, and also in the early period of Christianity. During the Middle Ages such disputations had as their objective the eventual conversion of the Jewish debaters. One of the most famous such public debates, lasting for 69 sessions, took place in 15th-century Spain, with 22 Rabbis representing Judaism, and the whole having the air of a theatrical spectacle.

DISSECTION. Talmudic teaching opposes any mutilation of a corpse, regarding it as a violation of the rights of the decedent. Permission to perform an autopsy has been granted, however, by the Israel Chief Rabbinate on conditions that such postmortems are conducted on the "bodies of persons who give their consent in writing, of their own free will during their lifetime, for anatomical dissections as required for medical studies, provided that the dissected parts be carefully preserved so as to be later buried with all due respect to Jewish law."

DIVINE RETRIBUTION. Belief that God rewards the righteous and punishes the wicked is one of the basic tenets of Judaism. Maimonides, in his "13 Articles of Faith," noted: "The Creator, blessed be he, rewards those who fulfill his commandments and punishes those who transgress against them." Nevertheless, the age-old question why the righteous suffer and the wicked prosper preoccupied the prophets and the Talmudic sages, many of whom came to the conclusion that the principal reward would be granted in the next world or in the Messianic era.

DIVINE REVELATION. Act by which God manifests himself miraculously to man or reveals his will through a vision. Such revelation is carried out to announce a prophecy or to offer guidance to man in fulfillment of a commandment. Places of revelation were considered sacred, and the Patriarchs built altars to mark the sites. Revelations came to the Patriarchs, Moses, the Prophets, and the prophets of other peoples, e.g., Balaam, as well as in dreams. Kabbalistic literature recounts numerous incidents of revelation to the righteous.

DIVORCE. (*Get* in Hebrew.) Dissolution of a marriage is produced by the issuance of a bill of divorcement. Although the Bible states that a woman can be divorced against her will, this has not been practicable since the rulings of Rabbi Gershom in the 11th century; it is possible today, but only under exceptional conditions. Judaism does not encourage divorce, but recognizes that where a marriage is totally impossible for the husband and wife, obstacles should not be placed in the way of a divorce. In Israel, matters of divorce are under the jurisdiction of Rabbinic courts (while Muslim and Christian divorce proceedings are handled in those communities' religious courts). Most Orthodox and Conservative Jews, and some Reform Jews, insist on obtaining a religious *get* in addition to a civil divorce.

DOGMA. The concept of an authoritative set of rules spelling out the tenets of Judaism is alien to Jewish tradition, which stresses the practices of Judaism as opposed to a rigid set of theological beliefs.

DOUBT. (*Safek* in Hebrew.) Where the law is not explicit or the facts are uncertain, Jewish law asserts that doubt exists. Generally, doubts with regard to Biblical law are resolved in keeping with a strict interpretation while those of Rabbinic origin are interpreted more leniently. In money matters a lenient attitude is preferred, as well as in matters that might endanger life. The thinking here is that Rabbinic de-

Scenes at a divorce. 1) Writing the get.
2) Reading it aloud. 3) Throwing the get to the
husband. 4) Husband throwing the get to the wife.

crees had to be based on cases where the evidence
was unmistakably clear.

DOWRY. (*Nedunyah* in Hebrew; *naden* in Yiddish.)
Property conveyed by the bride to her husband-to-be,
which could be in the form of movable or stationary
goods. In Biblical days it was customary for the groom
to pay a bride price (known as a mohar) for his future
wife, a custom still practiced by most Arabs. Traditionally the father of the bride provides the dowry, but
in the case of a poor girl communal funds were ex-

pected to be dipped into for this purpose. In the case of a divorce, the dowry must be returned to the wife. A husband is not allowed to sell his wife's immovable property without her agreement.

DREAM. Although the Bible viewed dreams as of great importance, only two of the Biblical personalities (Joseph and Daniel) are known to have been dream interpreters. The Talmud devotes considerable space to dreams and their interpretations, noting inter alia that a "man sees in a dream only what is suggested by his own thoughts." In ancient days, a person who had had a bad dream would fast for a day.

DRUNKENNESS. This social and moral illness was practically unknown among the Jews in Biblical and post-Biblical times, although there is one Talmudic reference stipulating that a person who is drunk is legally responsible for his actions—unless he has reached the state of total intoxication known to Lot. Aaron's two sons lost their lives, according to Rabbinic tradition, because they entered the sanctuary while drunk. It is regarded as permissible if not required to imbibe to such an extent on Purim that one is no longer able to distinguish between Mordecai and Haman. Rabbinic commentators have hastened to explain that this dictim is not to be taken too literally.

DUKHAN. (Hebrew for "platform.") Originally, a platform in the Holy Temple which the priests ascended to bless the congregation. The term is used today (as a verb) to describe the Kohanim (Jews of priestly descent) who bless the congregation, a practice in force primarily among Orthodox Jews.

DURESS. (*Oness* in Hebrew.) The Talmud teaches that a person is responsible for his actions only if he has freely initiated them. Thus a betrothed virgin who has been raped is free of all punishment, since she acted under duress. The concept is reserved largely to physical violence or matters dealing with a threat to life. An attempt to force one to commit one of the cardinal sins (idolatry, murder, or an adulterous or incestuous act) is to be resisted even if it leads to death. If a person, however, out of fear or under duress commits one of these transgressions, he is to remain unpunished.

DUTY. (*Chovah* in Hebrew.) A duty signifies a debt that must be paid to God or to one's fellow man, as distinct from a mitzvah, a commandment which generally indicates a commendable deed. The "duties of the heart," as explained by Ibn Pakuda, which led to a higher spiritual life, were distinct from the "duties of the limbs," which performed various ceremonial and practical acts.

DVAR TORAH. (Hebrew for "a word of Torah.") A concise Torah lesson that often accompanies a social or festive occasion, such as a group's meeting or a *seudah shlishit.*

DYBBUK. (Hebrew for "attachment.") A popular belief that the soul of a sinner enters the body of a living person; because of the gravity of the sins of these spirits, they were not permitted to undergo transmigration. The person possessed is generally regarded as having harbored hidden sins. The only way to rid the possessed person of the dybbuk was through exorcism, in a religious rite. Such rites, and the belief in a dybbuk, were known in Hasidic and kabbalistic sections of Jewry; there is no reference to such spirits in Jewish literature before the 17th century.

E

ECCLESIASTES. (*Koheleth* in Hebrew.) One of the five scrolls in the Holy Writings, the third of the three sections comprising the Jewish Bible (the first, the Torah, also called the Five Books of Moses, and the second, the Prophets, containing the prophets' works, while Psalms, Proverbs and the Five Scrolls are in the Holy Writings). The work consists of meditations of the writer, who has not found spiritual solace in faith or in the intellectual, but continues to strive toward understanding the purpose of life, despite its manifold problems ending in sickness and death. His pessimistic view is summarized in the well-known phrase "Vanity of vanities—all is vanity." The philosophy of Ecclesiastes, that nothing in life is really worthwhile since everything is preordained and nothing can be changed, is contrary to the rest of the Bible's teachings, which lay stress on justice and the eventual abolition of evil. Some of the early Rabbis opposed its inclusion in the Bible, but the tradition that it was the work of King Solomon during the latter part of his life helped to overcome their opposition. Scholars today believe it was composed in the 3d century B.C.E. It is read in the synagogue on the intermediate Sabbath of the feast of tabernacles (Sukkoth).

EDEN, GARDEN OF. (*Gan Eden* in Hebrew.) Genesis recounts that God "planted a garden eastward in Eden" in which Adam and Eve lived, but they suffered expulsion after eating from the tree of knowledge. There is a hint in Ezekiel of an ancient tradition that the wondrous garden that God planted in Eden was rich in beautiful trees bearing sweet fruit. Later literature adopted the name to denote the dwelling place of righteous souls after their departure from the body. In the Talmud distinction is made between the "Garden of Eden above and the Garden of Eden below: in the heavenly abode there is neither food nor drink, but the righteous sit with crowns on their heads, enjoying the glory of the divine presence."

EDUCATION. The obligation to instruct all the people in God's commandments is stressed frequently in the Bible. This religious education was at first a matter of parental duty and example, aided by folk tales and oral teachings. Indications exist that literacy was widespread in ancient Israel. After Ezra instituted regular public readings of the Torah, and the development of a cadre of scribes and scholars, new impetus was given to formal education. The Talmud reports the establishment of schools for boys at age 6. The concept of lifelong study of the Torah took hold through the ages and produced the high regard that scholarship has always enjoyed in the Jewish community. Most Jewish youngsters in the U.S. and other western countries receive a simultaneously secular and religious education.

EGLAH ARUFAH. (Hebrew for "beheaded heifer.") According to the Bible, if a corpse of a murdered man was found in the field (in Israel), and the identity of the murderer was unknown, the elders of the nearest town were instructed to bring a young heifer "which has not been wrought with and which had not drawn in the yoke," and to break its neck "in a rough valley which neither be plowed nor sown." Thereupon the elders were to wash their hands and recite, "Our hands have not shed this blood, neither have our eyes seen it." The Rabbis explained this unusual ceremony as follows: "Let the heifer which has never produced fruit be killed in a spot which has never produced fruit to atone for the death of a man who was debarred from producing fruit." The custom was discontinued after the number of murders grew in frequency.

EHAD MI YODEA. (Hebrew for "Who knows one?") Medieval hymn sung at the end of the Passover seder service by Ashkenazic Jews, consisting of 13 riddles. Believed to have been included so as to retain the interest of young children participating in the seder. The author is unknown.

EIN K'ELOHEYNU. (Hebrew for "There is none like our God.") Hymn praising God, of early origin, found in practically all prayer books. The hymn is an acrostic of the word "amen."

EINHORN, DAVID. Early Reform Rabbi; born in Germany, he led a congregation in Budapest and from 1855 on, spread the Reform movement in the U.S. He introduced Sunday services, denied the authority of the Talmud, initiated the use of organ music at services, and insisted that men uncover their heads during prayers. A prayer book that he composed omitted the hope for the return to Zion.

EL MALEH RACHAMIM. (Hebrew for "God, full of compassion.") Prayer beseeching rest for the souls of the departed. It is usually recited at a grave site after burial and recitation of the Yizkor memorial service for the dead, which is part of the Day of Atonement service, and is also included on Sukkoth, Passover, and Shavuoth.

ELDERS. Group of people with authority to rule the people or the state. The first reference is to Moses' appointing a group of elders: 70 elders were purportedly privileged to accompany him when he ascended Mount Sinai. Generally the elders were advisory rather than legislative. Eventually they were absorbed into the Sanhedrin, or Great Assembly.

ELIJAH. Prophet during the reigns of Ahab and Ahaziah, in the kingdom of Israel. Described in Scripture as a fearless, uncompromising defender of monotheism and a staunch fighter for moral principles. The Bible recounts that he ascended to heaven on a chariot of fire. He figures in Jewish tradition as the valiant defender of the Jewish people's covenant with God, and as such is the patron of circumcision and the

David Einhorn

guardian of Jewish children. (A special chair is set aside for him at every circumcision ceremony.) He is also regarded, according to the Prophet Malachi, as the harbinger of the Messiah.

ELIJAH'S CUP. An extra cup of wine is placed at the Passover seder table on the two nights of the holiday for Elijah the Prophet. Legend says that on Passover eve Elijah visits every Jewish household; during the seder service, every family opens the door, all present rise to welcome Elijah, and intone the verse: "Pour out your wrath on the nations that have not known you."

ELUL. 12th month of the Jewish religious year. During the days of the Second Temple, emissaries traveled abroad during Elul to inform Jews when to observe the upcoming New Year (which began the following month). For many generations Elul has been marked by preparation for the forthcoming High Holy Days. In Ashkenazic synagogues the shofar is sounded every morning after the daily service; among the Sephardim, the month is referred to as *rachamim* ("compassion"). Customarily, Jews visit the graves of their loved ones during the month, which coincides with August.

END OF DAYS. (*Ketz hayamim* in Hebrew.) Messianic era; the time of redemption. Regarded in Jewish thought as one of the unknowable mysteries; legend has it that when Jacob tried to tell his sons about the end of days, the divine presence left him. Through all the centuries of exile Jews have tried to compute the exact date of the end of days, but most Rabbis disapproved of the practice. The mystical kabbalists devoted much effort to trying to decipher the Bible, especially the Book of Daniel, for hints on when the Messianic era would come. Jewish tradition holds that the end of days will coincide with the Day of Judgment, with the war between Gog and Magog, the advent of the Messiah, the resurrection of the dead, and the establishment of the kingdom of God on earth.

EPHOD. Upper tunic worn by the High Priest in Bible times, to which was attached the breastplate containing the Urim and Thummim.

ERETZ ISRAEL. (Hebrew for, literally, "the Land of Israel.") The term was used widely throughout the Diaspora but has now largely been supplanted by the name of the state, Israel.

EREV. (Hebrew for "eve.") Sabbath and all Jewish holidays and festivals begin on the evening of the preceding day, at sunset. Hence *Erev Shabbat* ("Sabbath eve"), *Erev Yom Tov* ("holiday eve").

ERUV. (Hebrew for "blending.") General term for three types of Rabbinic laws designed to ease some of the stricter regulations in order to advance the sanctity of the Sabbath: (1) *Eruv hatzerot* permits the carrying of an object on the Sabbath in an area that is in general use by people, such as an alleyway. (2) *Eruv tehumim* does not permit one to leave one's place of residence on Sabbath, but it is deemed allowable if food has been placed at the destination beforehand, symbolizing that it too is one's residence. (3) *Eruv tavshilin* eases the rule that it is not permissible to prepare food on a festival day for the Sabbath, whenever cooking preparations began, even if only symbolically, on the preceding day.

ESHET CHAYIL. (Hebrew for "a woman of worth.") How the Book of Proverbs describes the ideal wife. The term is used today as an accolade for a Jewish woman who is an exemplary mother, wife, and communal worker.

ESSENES. Early Jewish religious sect that disappeared around the 1st century. Members were extremely uncompromising in observance of religious laws, including dietary, Sabbath, and purity regulations. Considered an ascetic and profoundly pious group (their name is believed to mean, in the Greek version of Aramaic, "the pious"), they looked forward to an imminent ushering in of the Messianic era. Their principal residence was along the Dead Sea shore; according to Josephus, one part of the sect practiced celibacy.

ESTHER, BOOK OF. One of the five scrolls of the Holy Writings, in the last of the three principal sections of the Bible. It is read in the synagogue on Purim eve and at morning services of the festival celebrating the defeat of Haman and his plan to commit genocide against the Jews who lived in the ancient Persian Empire. Although the historic accuracy of the story is open to question, Queen Esther and her cousin Mordecai have continued to be popular heroic figures in Jewish tradition.

Scroll of Esther, written and engraved on parchment. Holland, late 17th century.

ESTHER, FAST OF. On the day before Purim (the 13th of Adar), Esther's fasting before confronting Haman in front of her husband, King Ahasuerus, accusing the former of a diabolical plan to kill all the Jews in the latter's domain, is marked by the very observant as a fast day.

ETERNAL LIGHT. (*Ner tamid* in Hebrew.) Also known as the eternal lamp, it is found in almost every synagogue, directly above the ark housing the scrolls of the Law. Usually identifiable as a small bulb encased in a red globe, it is reminiscent of the Biblical injunction to have a light burning at all times in the Holy Temple, with only the purest of olive oil to be used.

ETHICAL WILLS. Primarily a custom that evolved in the Middle Ages, the writing of ethical wills to be left as a testament from father to son became a widespread practice among Jewish scholars. Some of the most famous are those of Rabbi Eleazar ben Judah of Worms, Rabbi Asher ben Yehiel, and Rabbi Sheftel. These ethical wills contained admonitions to the next generation stressing the importance of living morally, humbly, and adhering to the precepts of the Torah. Collections of ethical wills that have survived are still studied by advanced scholars of Judaica.

ETHICS. Jewish ethical teachings and the Jewish code of moral conduct are based on the Biblical principles of man's being created in the image of God and on the injunction to love one's neighbor as oneself. Hillel's famous summation of Judaism's ethical philosophy said: "What is hateful to you, do not unto thy fellow man." The *Ethics of the Fathers,* also called *Perek,* is devoted wholly to the teaching of ethical behavior for all people and in most conceivable situations. Another classic work of ethical instruction was written in the 18th century by the Italian Jewish scholar and poet Hayim Luzzato; it is called *Messilat Yesharim* ("Path of the Upright"). In the east European yeshivot, where Talmudic studies emphasized intellectual stimulation, Rabbi Israel Salanter achieved great renown by emphasizing the importance of ethical behavior as the primary goal of Jewish religious life.

ETROG. (Also known, among Yiddish-speaking Jews, as *esrog;* Hebrew for "citron.") One of the four species carried and symbolically shaken as part of the Sukkoth (feast of tabernacles) celebration. The citron, believed to be the "fruit of a goodly tree" referred to in the Bible, was widely accepted as a symbol of Jewry.

ETZ CHAYIM. (Hebrew for "tree of life.") The wooden rollers on which the scroll of the Law is rolled are called *atzei chaim* (pl.); the phrase is used to describe the Jewish way of life. *See also* Tree of Life.

EULOGY. (*Hesped* in Hebrew.) The first eulogies occurred in the Bible, when David paid final tributes to King Saul and to Jonathan. Most eulogies nowadays, in western countries, take place in the funeral chapel just before the deceased is taken to the cemetery for burial, but some, especially for Rabbis, scholars, and communal leaders, are held in the synagogue. During certain festivals, eulogies are not allowed.

EVIL EYE. (*Ain ha-ra* in Hebrew.) Ancient superstition mentioned in the Talmud and the kabbalah. It indicates that certain people can harm others by casting an envious or spiteful glance at them. The wearing of amulets to ward off such a possibility was widespread among simple folk in the Middle Ages. The popular Yiddish expression *kain ein n'hora* ("without the evil eye"), used after one refers to good tidings, indicates that the superstitious feeling is still in force.

EVIL TONGUE. (*L'shon ha-ra* in Hebrew.) Scandalbearing is prohibited in Judaism, based on the Biblical injunction that "you shall not go up and down as a talebearer among your people." Some Rabbis have said that slander is an offense even worse than the three cardinal sins. A person who listens to and accepts a slanderer's story is considered by the Rabbis as guilty as the talebearer himself.

EXCOMMUNICATION. Cutting off a Jew from the body of the Jewish community, and from all its rights and privileges, was carried out as punishment for a sin or to ensure compliance with community decisions. A mild form was a one-day (in Israel, seven-day) banishment, with the offender forced to retire to his home and refrain from contact with anyone. A stronger form of excommunication lasted a full month, during which the offender had to conduct himself as though he were a mourner. The most extreme form, known as herem, suspended the person from the community indefinitely, and was a step taken only in grave situations, amid Talmud-dictated ceremonies. One of history's most famous excommunications was that of the Jewish community in Amsterdam against Spinoza. With the exception of a few ultra-Orthodox groups, Jewish communities no longer practice this form of punishment.

EXODUS. Departure of the Israelite slaves from

Egyptian bondage, under the leadership of Moses, and their eventual settlement in Canaan, i.e., Palestine. Considered the beginning of the Jewish people's history as a nation. The Bible, the Passover seder, and the daily prayers refer to the exodus frequently, which the Rabbis interpret as stressing the importance of God-given freedom.

EXODUS, BOOK OF. Second book of the Five Books of Moses (also known as the Torah or the Pentateuch). Containing the Ten Commandments and many basic precepts of Judaism, it also lists the celebration of three historic festivals and the observance of the Sabbath.

EZEKIEL. Third of the three Major Prophets, found in the second section of the Bible. A seer of the Babylonian exile, in the 6th century B.C.E., Ezekiel described the divine summons to his soul and body, and prophesied the eventual return of the Jewish exiles to Jerusalem and their reconciliation with God. He emphasized the importance of individual adherence to the laws of Judaism. His vision of the dry bones, voicing confidence in Israel's eventual regeneration, remains very poignant to the Jewish community.

EZRA. Priest and scribe. He led some 2000 Jewish exiles from Babylonia back to Jerusalem, instituted religious reforms, including the annulment of mixed marriages between Jews and pagans, and set about teaching the Torah's precepts to large masses of people. He also preached strict observance of the Sabbath, and resurrected the festival of tabernacles. Tradition attributes him with being the prime founder of the Great Assembly, which laid the foundations for a more advanced form of Jewish religious life. Talmud also notes that he made the final decision on the precise contents of the written Torah, and credits him with introducing square Hebrew script.

EZRAT NASHIM. (Hebrew for "women's court.") Section of a synagogue set aside for women worshipers. Such sections are found today only in Orthodox synagogues, since Conservative and Reform congregations have banished separate seating.

F

FALSE WITNESS. Witnesses who deliberately give untrue evidence in order to incriminate a defendant are considered to be breaking a Biblical commandment. The prohibition against the giving of false testimony is interpreted in Judaism as including slander and defamation against whole peoples or faiths, as well as testimony taken in a court of law.

FAMILY. Concept that dates to early Bible times in Jewish teaching. The first tribes were regarded as groups of families, while the first of the 613 basic precepts of Judaism—"Be fruitful and multiply"—was seen by the Rabbis as stressing the primary importance of establishing and maintaining a family. Jewish tradition abounds with the congeniality of family life, which is largely patriarchal in nature. Although in Bible times concubines were an acceptable social institution, especially where the wife was barren, the trend in Judaism was toward monogamy, which was adopted by western civilization. Considerable emphasis was laid throughout Jewish history on the concept of family purity (*taharat hamishpachah*), which forbade illicit relationships and strove for ritual cleanliness, modesty, and a general ambience of sanctity of the family.

FARBREINGUNG. (Yiddish for "a joyous celebration.") Hasidic festival in which the group's Rebbe speaks at some length on a Torah subject, followed by group singing and sometimes dancing and refreshments.

FAST. Abstaining from eating is carried out as a form of expiation of sins, as a sign of mourning, and as supplication for divine compassion. Major fasts call for not only avoiding food and drink but also abstinence from sexual intercourse; the Orthodox do not wear leather shoes on Yom Kippur, considered the most solemn fast day. Most fast days mark tragic days in Jewish history, notably the 9th of Av, when the Holy Temple was destroyed. Some ultra-Orthodox Jews fast every Monday and Thursday, on the theory that such self-punishment will lead them to a higher spiritual plane.

FATALISM. A totally fatalistic attitude is not compatible with traditional Judaism, which emphasizes man's free will while at the same maintaining that everything is in God's hands. This seeming paradox is explained as God being ready to be influenced by a person's prayers, repentance of sins, and execution of good works.

FATHER. The rights of a father in Jewish law, while his children are minors, are almost unlimited. While one of the Ten Commandments demands respect for parents, a father at the same time is obligated to his children, specifically (citing the Talmud), "to circumcise his son, teach him Torah, teach him a trade, and marry him off." Fathers are also required to maintain their children during their minor years. A child, on the other hand, who is ordered by his parents to sin against the laws of Judaism, must defy them. According to the Talmud, proof of paternity is not required—if a man claims a child as his own, he is to be believed. A father may punish a child only while he is a minor, and legally his responsibility toward his child is considered completed when the child reaches majority.

FEAR OF GOD. Jewish religious teaching emphasizes repeatedly the need to "fear" or be in awe of God. The Bible says that fear of God is "the beginning of knowledge" and "the beginning of wisdom." Rabbi Antigonus summed up the Jewish attitude by asserting that one should serve God without any thought of reward, but "let the fear of heaven be upon you." The Rabbis of the Talmud added: "Everything is in the hands of heaven except for the fear of heaven."

FENCE. (S'yag in Hebrew.) Symbolic fence around the observance of Jewish law. Mentioned in the Talmud as a safeguard to ensure the observance of Biblical commandments.

FESTIVAL PRAYERS. Services on the festivals are basically similar to those of the daily schedule, except that an additional (musaf) service is added in the morning. (It is also added on the Sabbath.) On Yom

Kippur, a section of the service known as neilah is appended, and is recited just before the conclusion of the service. Various small additions are made on the respective festivals, relative to their observance.

FESTIVALS. The Torah enumerates five festivals to be observed during the year—Passover, Shavuoth, and Sukkoth (known as pilgrim festivals, when ancient Israelites made pilgrimages to the Holy Temple in Jerusalem), Rosh Hashanah, and Yom Kippur. Dancing, singing, and rejoicing marked the celebration of these special days, while Yom Kippur was reserved as a day of personal and Temple purification. The pilgrim festivals combine both historical and agricultural motifs: Passover denotes the beginning of spring and marks the exodus from Egypt; Shavuoth commemorates the harvest of the first fruits, and simultaneously the traditional anniversary of the revelation at Mount Sinai; Sukkoth, the time of the last harvest of the year, also serves to remind Jews of the time when their forebears wandered in the desert for 40 years after the exodus from Egypt, living all the time in tabernacles or booths. Traditionally, and by Biblical injunction, celebration of the festivals must include the needy, strangers, slaves, orphans, and widows. Relatively recent festivals added to the Jewish calendar include Hanukkah, Purim, and Israel Independence Day.

FIRST FRUITS. (*Bikkurim* in Hebrew.) The Bible decrees that the first fruits—fruits of the trees and vegetables as well as the first catch of the fisherman or hunter—should be brought to the Holy Temple. Traditionally, pilgrims to Jerusalem brought their first-fruit offerings amid much rejoicing and ceremony, including the singing of Psalm 30. After the destruction of the Temple the Rabbis decreed that acts of charity could be substituted, particularly support of impoverished scholars. In Israel there has been a renewal of the festive first-fruits celebrations, with children bedecked in garlands symbolically transporting baskets of new fruits.

FIRSTBORN (*Bechor* in Hebrew.) By Biblical command, the firstborn son is entitled to inherit a double portion of his father's estate. A firstborn son also inherits certain hereditary offices, provided he is deemed worthy. (Neither a posthumously born son nor one delivered by caesarean section is regarded as a firstborn.)

FIRSTBORN, REDEMPTION OF (*Pidyon ha-ben* in Hebrew.) By Biblical law, all firstborn sons on the mother's side were to be dedicated to God's service, commemorating the deliverance of the Israelite firstborn sons at the time the Egyptians' sons were slain, just before the exodus. In ancient times the firstborn son could usually be released from this obligation by redemption, however, usually through the payment of five shekels to the priest 30 days after birth. (Since members of the priestly tribe, the Kohanim, and the Levites are consecrated to serving God, the law of redemption does not apply to them. Today the *Pidyon ha-ben* ceremony is still in force, usually serving as the occasion for a festive gathering.

FIVE BOOKS OF MOSES. The Torah, also known as the Pentateuch, the first of the three parts of the Jewish Bible. The five books are Genesis, Exodus, Leviticus, Numbers, and Deuteronomy.

FLESH. The word as used in the Bible refers to the human body and to a kind of food. Eating of animals is limited, according to the dietary laws, to named species, which must be slaughtered within accepted norms. Traditionally the Rabbis did not look upon mankind (another meaning of the word "flesh") as innately sinful, but recognized the human frailties and the temptations of the flesh, teaching that "flesh" should not be negated but rather directed to sanctification and uplifting.

FLOGGING. A person who violated a negative commandment where there is no mention of the death penalty was, according to the Bible, to be flogged 13 times on the chest and 26 times on the back. (It was left to Rabbinic initiative to decide if a flagrant violator of the positive commandments was also to be flogged.) The practice has long been abandoned.

FLOOD. As described in Genesis, God created a massive deluge to destroy mankind for its sinful ways. Noah alone, together with his immediate family, was to be saved by building an ark in which he would take aboard pairs of all fauna. The Flood continued for 150 days.

FORBIDDEN FOODS. Opposite of kosher food. Known as terefah. (See also Dietary Laws.)

FORGIVENESS. Confession of sinfulness, repentance, and resolution to abstain from repetition of the original transgression are the accepted Jewish conditions for attaining forgiveness from God. For sins committed against a fellow man the sinner must additionally rectify any wrongdoing and obtain the injured party's pardon.

FOUR DEATHS. Members of a Bet Din, in Talmudic days, were authorized to impose four forms of capital punishment, and these came to be known as Arba Mitot Beth Din ("the four deaths of the court"): stoning, burning, beheading, and strangulation. Executed criminals were buried on the day of death, and the implements used in their execution were buried with them.

FOUR QUESTIONS. (Arba kushiyot in Hebrew; fir kashes in Yiddish.) At the Passover seder the youngest son present asks his father four traditional questions, all related to the customs and rituals of the holiday. The reading of the Haggadah is considered a response to the questions. The first question begins with the phrase "Mah nishtanah halailah hazeh?" ("Why is this night [of Passover] different?")

FOUR SPECIES. (Arba minim in Hebrew.) Four plants—the lulav ("palm branch"), etrog ("citron"), hadas ("myrtle"), and arava ("willow")—are used during colorful holding and waving ceremonies on Sukkoth, in accordance with Biblical command. There are many interpretations for the use of these, including analogies between the four species and four different kinds of people, and also comparisons between the species and parts of the body. Scholars ascribe the ceremony to ancient rituals beseeching the Almighty for rain. During the festival, worshipers carry the etrog and lulav in a procession around the synagogue, chanting a festival prayer.

FOUR TRUSTEES. (*Arbaah shomrim* in Hebrew.) Talmudic law differentiates four kinds of trustees: (1) an unpaid trustee, who is responsible for the property but is not liable if he has been guarding properly and there is nonetheless a loss; (2) a paid trustee, who is responsible if the object he is protecting is lost or stolen; (3) a lessee, who uses the property himself and pays a fee; and (4) a borrower who uses it without payment—he is responsible even if the damage occurred in conditions that he was unable to avert. Trustee laws appear in the Bible, and are extensively elaborated on in the Talmud.

FRAUD. The Bible enumerates harsh penalties against fraud, including false weights and measures. Fraud annuls all contracts and entitles the injured party to damages. The purchaser of a faulty article must be told beforehand of the damage, or the sale is deemed fraudulent.

FREEDOM. Although slavery was practiced in ancient Israel, as well as throughout the world at the time, the principle of national and individual freedom was considered a divine gift. The Bible provides for automatic freedom of all Jewish slaves in the Jubilee year; a slave who had succeeded in fleeing from his master was, according to the Bible, not to be returned but to "dwell with thee"; a Jewish slave who could go free and nevertheless elected to remain in servitude was to have his earlobe pierced—a symbol seen by the Rabbis as chastisement for a Jew who preferred "security" to freedom. The principal theme of Passover is a reaffirmation of national freedom, and each seder celebrant is told to regard himself as "though he had himself gone out of Egypt."

GABBAI. (Hebrew for, literally, "a collector.") Those who collected taxes were scorned, but charity collectors were held in high regard, their honesty considered unassailable. Nevertheless, the Talmud advises that in order to avoid any suspicion charity collectors should work in pairs. Today, a gabbai in a synagogue is generally an usher, and sometimes is given the responsibility for choosing those who are honored by being called to the reading of the Torah.

GAM ZO LE-TOVAH. (Hebrew for, literally, "This too is for the good.") Phrase used when something untoward has occurred and someone wishes to demonstrate his faith in Providence, and confidence that in the long run everything will turn out for the best.

GAMBLING. The Bible makes no reference to games of chance or gambling, Under the influence of the Greeks and later the Romans, Jews took part in such games, especially dice throwing, which led to stormy opposition from the Rabbis. Jewish law states that gambling debts cannot be claimed by law. (The Talmud subsequently made a distinction between professional gamblers and those for whom gambling is an avocation.) Jewish communal records of the Middle Ages indicate that gambling was a popular pastime.

GAON. (Hebrew; translatable as "excellency" or "eminence," although in modern Hebrew it means "a genius.") Used for the heads of leading academies. Gaonim (pl.) flourished for many centuries, writing responsa to religious problems and maintaining high levels of scholarship in schools of advanced Jewish studies. In more recent times, truly outstanding scholars and Jewish religious leaders (e.g., the Gaon of Vilna) have been accorded this distinctive appellation.

GARTEL. (Yiddish for "girdle.") Some Hasidic Jews, particularly at prayer, wear a gartel to separate the upper from the lower part of the body; it is also symbolic of the Biblical injunction that encourages the "girding of the loins" in God's service.

GEDALIAH, FAST OF. The day after Rosh Hashanah (the 3d of Tishri) is a fast day, marking the murder of Gedaliah, son of Ahikam, who was named governor of Judah by Nebuchadnezzar following the destruction of the First Temple in the 6th century B.C.E. The murder, by Ishmael ben Nathanya, a member of the royal family, brought in its wake the departure of the Jews remaining in the country and the end of Jewish self-government.

GEHENNA. (Also called Gehinom.) Place of darkness and utter void where the souls of the wicked are punished and purified, while the souls of the righteous dwell in the Garden of Eden. The word comes from the valley of Ben Hinnom, south of Jerusalem, where child sacrifices were offered to Moloch by ancient idol worshipers. Talmudic legends detail the location, size, and divisions of Gehenna, where the wicked souls will suffer burning.

GELILAH. (Hebrew for "rolling.") In Ashkenazic synagogues, after the reading of the Law is completed, a member of the congregation is called upon for the honor of gelilah, i.e., rolling the open scroll to a closed position. A corollary honor is the lifting of the scroll of the Law (see hagbahah).

GEMAR HATIMAH TOVAH. Traditional greeting extended between Rosh Hashanah and Yom Kippur. Since a person's fate for the new year is written on Rosh Hashanah and sealed on Yom Kippur, the greeting expresses hope for a "final good sealing."

GEMARA. Comment on and discussions surrounding the Mishnah. The Gemara and Mishnah together comprise the Talmud. There is a Palestinian and a Babylonian Talmud, with separate Gemara sections for each Mishnah, but some tractates have come down from post-Biblical times without the appropriate Gemara.

GEMATRIAH. System whereby each Hebrew letter has a numerical value. It has led many Rabbis and commentaries to seek out words or word combinations that would total particular phrases in homiletic lessons. The use of gematriah was widespread among the mystical sects in Jewry.

GEMILUT HESED. Broadly translated, the concept denotes various forms of benevolent material and moral assistance without reward. Under this category are loans without interest or collateral to needy individuals, visiting the sick, helping an orphaned bride to a suitable marriage, and the like. The Talmud teaches that "he who has occupied himself with Torah but not with the performance of gemilut hesed is as though he had no God." The concept is considered on a higher plane than charity, which is restricted to giving to the poor, the living, and in kind, while gemilut hesed is unlimited and can include acts of service, honoring the dead, and helping a rich person in need of moral or spiritual bolstering. Most Jewish communities maintain some form of gemilut hesed groups.

GENESIS. First of the Five Books of Moses (also known as the Torah or the Pentateuch). It includes an account of the creation of the world by God, the story of mankind beginning with Adam, and the history of the Patriarchs (Abraham, Isaac, and Jacob) up to the death of Joseph.

GENIZAH. (Hebrew for "hiding.") A storeroom or hiding place in a synagogue for the safekeeping of worn-out sacred works, including Bibles, prayer books, copies of the Talmud, and the like. The most famous of such storerooms was the genizah found in the Cairo synagogue in the latter part of the 19th century, which housed manuscripts and rare books going back more than 1000 years. Most of the Cairo genizah materials were transferred gradually to various western libraries. The storerooms in the Qumran caves near the Dead Sea where the famous Dead Sea scrolls were found can also be called a genizah.

GENTILE. Usual English translation of the Hebrew word *goy* ("non-Jew"). A Jew, according to Jewish religious law, is one who is either born of a Jewish mother or has converted to the Jewish faith; all others are termed Gentiles. Gentiles are divided in Jewish teaching among those who are idol worshipers or pagans and those who have accepted the belief in one God. A resident stranger who believes in one God and has accepted the seven Noachian Laws (q.v.) has defined rights in the community. The Rabbis taught that "the pious of all the nations of the world have a share in the world to come." Maimonides defined these people as Gentiles who have accepted the seven laws of Noah as divine revelation.

GER. (Hebrew for "stranger.") Convert to the Jewish faith. The term originally referred to non-Jews living in Israel. There is a distinction between the *ger toshav*, the resident stranger who has accepted the Noachian Laws, and the *ger tzedek*, the convert of righteousness who has adopted Judaism and is regarded as a Jew in every respect.

GERIZIM. Highest of the Ephraim hills, located south of Nablus, the ancient Biblical city of Shechem. When the Samaritans were not permitted to join in the building of the Second Temple, they built their own sanctury on this hill, which to this day is the site of their chief ritual, the sacrifice of the Paschal lamb.

GERSHOM BEN JUDAH. Known throughout the Jewish world as *Meor-Ha-Golah* ("light of the Diaspora"), he was the leading Talmudic scholar in the 10th and 11th centuries in western Europe, and established the bases for subsequent Jewish scholarship that flourished in the French and German provinces. Many of his commentaries are included in Rashi's interpretations of the Talmud.

GET. *See* Divorce.

GEZERAH. (Hebrew for "decree.") Rabbinic prohibition. Opposite of a takkanah, a positive ruling. Gezerah came to be used to describe anti-Jewish decrees and persecutions.

GHETTO. Separate section set aside for the residence of Jews, generally enclosed by a wall. The word probably derives from the *geto nuovo* (Italian for "new quarter") established for the Jews in Venice in the 16th century. Despite overcrowding and generally abrasive features, the ghetto was considered by some Rabbis and scholars as a positive development, since it discouraged assimilation by Jews into the larger Gentile society and helped foster a stricter observance of religious life. Religious law in the ghetto often was expanded to include civil law, so

"Ghetto of Lublin," etching by Lionel S. Reiss.
United States, 20th century.

that the area became a self-contained community within a larger city, where Judaism could be followed to the letter of the law.

GIFTS TO THE POOR. Torah-ordered gifts to the poor, such as gleanings of the field and the *ma'aser ani* ("tithe for the poor"). Although the tithe could be earmarked for a specific individual, this was not true of gleanings of the harvest—they had to be left for anyone in need, who could pick up whatever was left after the reapers had departed.

GILGUL. (Hebrew for, literally, "rolling.") Mystical belief in the transmigration of souls. One such belief holds that souls go through various human bodies; another, called *gilgul mehilot*, says that in the Messianic era, when the dead will be resurrected, they will roll in subterranean movements till they reach Israel, while those buried in the Holy Land will simply rise up again. These concepts are not found in the Bible or the Talmud, and were dismissed by Maimonides and others.

GIVING OF THE LAW. (*Mattan Torah* in Hebrew.) Revelation at Mount Sinai, when the Torah was given to the Jewish people via Moses. Tradition says that not only the Ten Commandments but also the whole of the Torah Law, as well as the oral law, were transmitted to the Jews at the time. The holiday of Shavuoth celebrates the giving of the law, as well as the harvest of first fruits. While Orthodox Jews believe that God literally gave the Ten Commandments to Moses on Mount Sinai, Reform Jews maintain that Moses was divinely inspired, and Conservative Jews take a somewhat in-between attitude, although formally they too accept revelation as a literal event.

GOD. In Judaism, God's existence is taken for granted from the very first words in the Bible; no need is felt to prove his existence. Judaism regards God as the Supreme Being; as Creator of the Universe; as Judge and Ruler of history; as the Supreme Lawgiver. Some Biblical nouns help to explain God's position— Father, Shepherd, Judge, King. Judaism differs from other early religions in that God is conceived as having no corporeal form, no relatives, and no human needs; on the contrary, he is the sovereign ruler of nature, which is totally dependent on him. Since there are no other divine beings, this concept gave rise to the idea of monotheism. Judaism believes that the Jewish people enjoy a special relationship to God, but if Jews fail to abide by his commandments, they are admonished by his prophets. Although the Bible teachings are meant to transform the Jewish people into a holy nation, God is the Lord of all peoples, not of the Jews alone.

GOG AND MAGOG. Gog, of the land of Magog, according to Ezekiel, will battle against the forces of God when the Jews have been gathered into their country. The vision says that Gog will come with many peoples from the north and rise up against Israel, to take spoils, but that God will come "with pestilence and blood" and pour down on him and his bands "an overflowing rain and great hailstones, fire, and brimstone." Then the name of God will be known among all peoples, who will regard him as the true God. Thus Gog in Jewish tradition symbolizes Israel's archetypal enemy, and the battle will immediately precede the Messianic period. Jewish tradition believes that only after this victory will there be full redemption of the Jewish people.

GOLDEN CALF. (*Egel hazahav* in Hebrew.) Constructed by the Israelites at the foot of Mount Sinai, when Moses failed to come down quickly from the mountain. When Moses descended the mountain and saw the golden calf (made up of the Israelites' golden ornaments), he smashed the twin tablets of the law and ordered the calf destroyed. The term has come to represent any object of idolatrous or non-Jewish worship that deflects the Jews from their traditional path of religious life.

GOMEL. Special blessing of thanksgiving, recited by someone who has survived a dangerous experience (a difficult journey, or a serious illness). It is usually recited on the first Sabbath after the event, when the individual is called to the reading of the Torah. The blessing is based on Psalm 107.

GOVERNMENT, PRAYER FOR. Prayer for the government under which a particular Jewish community lives has been a customary practice since the 14th century, and is based on Jeremiah's teaching ("Seek the peace of the city where I have caused you to be carried captive, and pray for it unto the Lord"), and a Talmudic addition, instructing that Jews should "pray for the welfare of the government." Most

American congregations include a special prayer for the government at the weekly Sabbath service, following reading of the Law.

GOY. (Hebrew for "a people.") Although the term as used in the Bible includes any people, and was used also in reference to the Jews, it has come to mean a non-Jew, or Gentile.

GRACE AFTER MEALS. (*Birkat ha-mazon* in Hebrew.) Religious law requires the recitation of grace after eating a meal that includes bread. The rite differs from an individual reciting grace to that of a group of at least three adult male Jews, when certain additions are made. Additions to the daily grace ritual are also made at Sabbath meals and on holidays.

GREAT ASSEMBLY. *See* Sanhedrin.

GREETINGS. The Talmud states that whoever greets another first demonstrates genuine piety. It is customary to greet fellow Jews on the Sabbath with the phrase *"Shabbat shalom"* ("A Sabbath of peace"), on Saturday night, at the Sabbath's conclusion, with *"Shavuah tov"* ("A good week"), on holidays, *"Chag same-ach"* ("Happy holiday"), and on Rosh Hashanah, *"L'shana tovah tikatevu"* ("May you be inscribed for a good year"). After one concludes a religious duty, such as being called to the Torah, he is greeted with *"Yishar koach"* ("May your strength increase"). The popular phrase *"Mazal tov,"* which translates best as "Congratulations," is reserved for special occasions, such as birthdays, bar and bat mitzvahs, and weddings. Upon entering the home of a mourner it is traditional to refrain from all greetings, including even a simple hello or, on departing, goodbye.

GROGGER. A noisemaker or rattle traditionally whirled to create noise by children attending Purim eve services when the Book of Esther is read; the noise is made upon hearing the name of the enemy of the Jews, Haman, who plotted to destroy all the Jews, but whose plans were revealed and thwarted by Queen Esther and her cousin Mordecai. The custom has been in force since the 13th century. Some eastern Jewish communities used to knock two stones together or stomp their feet to make the necessary noise at the mention of Haman's name.

GUILDS. In the Middle Ages, craftsmen's guilds were organized on a religious basis, with all Jews automatically excluded. Jews nevertheless had their own guild counterparts, some of which had a long history (there is a Biblical mention of groups of goldsmiths and merchants). In the east European shtetl, Jews who were tailors, cobblers, porters, etc., sometimes maintained special synagogues where the degree of learning was often markedly lower than at synagogues of the noncraftsmen, who presumably had more time to study.

HABAD. Acronym made up of three Hebrew words: *hochma* ("wisdom"), *binah* ("understanding"), and *daat* ("knowledge"). A popular segment of the Hasidic movement is known as Habad, also known as the Lubavich Hasidim. The philosophy of the movement stresses constant communion with God and intense feeling and concentration during prayer services. The Habad movement is an activist group, i.e., they are dedicated to winning new adherents among Jews, especially the young, who have not been exposed to intensive religious instruction.

HAD GADYA. Concluding song at the Passover seder service.

HAFTARAH. Prophetic portion read in the synagogue immediately after the weekly Sabbath reading of the Torah; it is also read on holidays and festivals. The selection usually has some reference to the Biblical portion, but sometimes it deals with a historical event. Bar and bat mitzvah youngsters traditionally read the haftarah aloud as part of their formal accession to religious majority.

HAGBAHAH. (Hebrew for "elevating.") The honor of elevating the scroll of the Law, upon conclusion of the reading at services, is usually accorded to a person

Four Rabbis. A full page miniature from the
Erna Michael Haggadah. Germany, Middle Rhine, c. 1400.

who is physically able to raise the Torah over his
head, if only for a minute, so that the congregants
can glimpse the words. When the Torah is raised, the
congregants rise and do not resume sitting until the
Torah has been lowered to the lap of the hagbahah
designee. It is then rolled together, tied, and its cover
replaced by the person designated as gelilah.

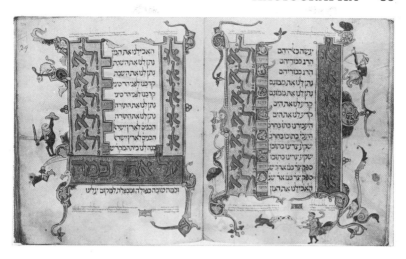

The poem *Dayyeinu* in a double page from the
Rylands Spanish Haggadah. Spain, late 14th century.

HAGGADAH. (Hebrew for "narration.") The book
used for the Passover service or seder includes a brief
description of the exodus from Egypt, appropriate
Biblical selections, praise of God for having wrought
the miracle of liberation, and hopes for full and future
redemption. The traditional four questions recited by
the youngest seder participant are answered by
reading the Haggadah. Part of the reading takes
place, amid various rituals, before the main meal,
and part afterward. In addition to specific references
to the matzah (unleavened bread) and maror (bitter
herbs, symbolizing the Israelites' bitter lives of en-
slavement), there is frequent singing of traditional
tunes, and the head of the house interpolates current
events to show the relevance of the Passover message, with its emphasis on freedom. Through the
centuries, thousands of versions of the Haggadah
have been printed, each reflecting a specific time or
place, e.g., there were Haggadahs circulating among
Jews in some of the Nazi concentration camps,
among Jewish military units in distant regions in
World War II, and more recently, secret Haggadahs
among Jews in the Soviet Union who were un-
officially forbidden to observe the ancient holiday.

HAGIOGRAPHA. Third and last section of the Bible,

also known as the Holy Writings, or *Ketuvim* in Hebrew, comprised of Psalms, Proverbs, Job, Song of Songs, Ruth, Lamentations, Ecclesiastes, Esther, Daniel, Ezra, Nehemiah, and Chronicles.

HAHAM. (Hebrew for "sage.") Among the Sephardic Jews, Haham is the title used for a fully ordained Rabbi. The same term was used in the Sanhedrin, where the Nasi was the president, the Av Bet Din the chief judge, and the third-ranking members were called Hahamin (pl.). Today, among Yiddish-speaking Jews, the term is often used to describe a sagacious child.

HAKHNASSAT KALLAH. Custom of communal responsibility for "bringing in the bride," when the young woman is too poor to provide a dowry for a prospective groom. It is a commandment considered even more important than Torah study, and is fulfilled secretly so that the bride does not know the identity of her benefactors.

HAKKAFOT. (Hebrew for "circuits.") During Simhat Torah, at the end of the Sukkoth festival, the scrolls of the Law are removed from the holy ark and carried around the synagogue seven times, amid singing and dancing, with children often following the procession carrying flags. The celebration coincides with the yearly completion of the reading of the Torah, i.e., the entire Pentateuch has been read aloud at weekly services; upon completion, another reading cycle is begun.

HALACHAH. (Hebrew for "law.") Jewish religious law which also encompasses ethical, civil, and criminal matters. Halachah is based first and foremost on Biblical commands, and these are followed—in degree of authority—by interpretations of the Torah, oral traditions, Rabbinic decrees issued in specific circumstances, and laws based on popular custom. The Mishnah section of the Talmud was the first formal code of Jewish law; the *Shulchan Aruch* is the code most often referred to today as the accepted code. Reform Judaism does not consider itself bound by the Halachah.

HALITZAH. *See* Levirate Marriage.

HALLAH. Sabbath and holiday loaf of bread, white and often braided. The word refers to the ancient commandment by which housewives were to set aside a portion of the bread they baked for the use of the priest. After the destruction of the Temple, the law was amended and women were to burn the piece set aside. In modern times, the baking of home-made hallot (pl.) has become a popular practice.

HALLEL. Group of psalms recited at synagogue services during Passover, Shavuoth, Sukkoth, Hanukkah and on Rosh Hodesh, the new month.

HALLELUYAH. (Hebrew for "Praise the Lord.") Exclamation found frequently in Psalms. During the Talmudic era it was the congregational response during the recitation of certain prayers. The word has been widely used in Christian worship services and hymns.

HALUKKAH. (Hebrew for "distribution.") During the 18th, 19th, and early 20th centuries, pious Jews living in four "holy cities" in Palestine (Jerusalem, Hebron, Safed, and Tiberias) subsisted on financial support from Jewish communities around the world. Although the practice has attenuated, there are still Orthodox Jews in the U.S. who forward funds to small clusters of Jews in Israel who devote their time to religious studies.

HAMAKOM YENACHEM. (Hebrew for "May God comfort.") Opening words of the traditional greeting offered a mourner who has just sustained a loss.

HAMETZ. (Hebrew for "leavened bread.") Eating leavened bread, or hametz, is prohibited during the Passover holiday, in memory of the Israelites' exodus from Egypt. (Because of their hasty departure for freedom, they could not wait for their dough to rise and thus ate matzah, or unleavened bread.) In preparation for Passover it is customary to ritually remove the hametz from the house and burn it. Housewives who store their non-Passover food products and utensils during the holiday also "sell" their hametz to a non-Jew for a nominal sum, in a ceremony indicating that they technically do not own the proscribed products during the holiday season. Nowadays, families designate their Rabbi to sell the hametz for them, and he in turn transacts such a sale, often to a non-Jewish neighbor or member of the synagogue staff. The alleged sale is canceled immediately after the holiday. Grain stored in Israel government warehouses, and other hametz products in the possession of army and other government installations are also "sold" in this manner, usually to an Arab.

The kindling of the eight lights of the Hanukkah menorah.

HANUKKAH. (Hebrew for "dedication.") Festival commenorating the rededication of the Holy Temple by the Maccabees in 165 B.C.E., three years after it was desecrated by Antiochus. Tradition says that the Maccabees found a cruse of oil that was supposed to last only a day but continued to burn for eight days, when a fresh supply could be prepared—hence the kindling of the eight lights of the Hanukkah menorah (a ninth light is the shammash, which is used to light the others). "Rock of Ages" (*Maoz Tzur* in Hebrew), a hymn of praise to God, is sung after each night's lighting of the candles. Today, in the United States especially, it has become customary to use an electric Hanukkah menorah (known as a Hanukkiyah), which is placed in the front window for all to see.

HAROSET. Part of the Passover seder table requirements. Haroset is a mixture (generally) of ground nuts, apple, and cinammon, dipped in wine, recalling the mortar used by the ancient Israelites when they labored as slaves in pre-exodus Egypt.

HARVEST FESTIVALS. Passover, Shavuoth, Sukkoth, the three Biblical pilgrim festivals, are also referred to as harvest festivals. The last festival, falling in the early autumn, is believed to have been the example followed by the Pilgrims in America when they established Thanksgiving Day.

HASIDISM. 18th-century east European religious-mystical-revival movement that spread to nearly all parts of the world; today, best exemplified by the Lubavich movement. A Hasid (Hebrew for "pious one") stresses religious fervor and devotion to good deeds, strict adherence to all laws, customs, and traditions, shunning of such modern conveniences as television, and emphasis on the spiritual life—but all in the ambience of religious singing and dancing. Although study is encouraged, followers of the Hasidic movement are urged to approach Judaism through the heart far more than through the mind. In major U.S. cities Lubavich Hasidim may be seen approaching fellow Jews (never non-Jews), urging them to pray, observe the rules of kashruth, and return to a life of religious observance.

HASKALAH. (Hebrew for "enlightenment.") Movement that originated in central Europe in the 18th century. It encouraged Jews steeped in exclusively religious studies to broaden their knowledge of the world through secular studies. Haskalah opposed the exclusive dependence of Jews on the Talmud and the Bible as suitable subjects for study, and sought to bring the fruits of the new European emancipation to the Jewish masses.

HASMONEANS. Family name of the priestly family, popularly known as the Maccabees, who organized the revolt against the ancient Syrians, leading to the cleansing and rededication of the Holy Temple. Their efforts are commemorated in the annual Hanukkah festival.

HATAN TORAH. (Hebrew for "bridegroom of the Law.") Name given to the person called to the reading of the last portion of the Torah at Simhat Torah, when the annual reading is concluded and begun anew. *Hatan bereishit* ("bridegroom of Genesis") is the person who is called to the reading of the first section of the Torah.

HAVDALAH. (Hebrew for "differentiation.") Ceremony and special prayer recited at the conclusion of the Sabbath (and festivals), denoting the cutoff of the sacred day from the mundane workday that follows. The ceremony includes the kindling of a special, braided candle, and sniffing of spices, signifying the hope for a materially rewarding week.

HAZAK. (Hebrew for "Be strong.") Exclamation recited in unison by the congregation immediately following the reading of one of the Five Books of Moses (the Torah). The full phrase reads: *"Hazak, hazak, v'nithazek"* ("Be strong, be strong, and let us be strengthened").

HAZZAN. *See* Cantor.

HEAD COVERING. Orthodox Jews (males) keep their head covered at all times, while Conservative Jews cover their heads at religious services and usually at Sabbath and festival-meals, when a blessing is recited. Reform Jews generally pray bare-

Silver spice containers for the havdalah ceremony.

headed. Although there is no Biblical or other legal basis for head covering, it is a custom that has taken on the force of law today. Some young Jews especially wear small skullcaps in public to exhibit their commitment to Judaism. *See also* Yarmulke.

HEBREW. Biblical term for Israelite, and the word used for the language of the Bible and of modern Israel. Popularly believed to originate from the word *ever* ("one who crossed over"), referring to Abraham, who came from the "other side of the Jordan River."

HEBREW UNION COLLEGE. The principal Rabbinic seminary for Reform Rabbis, with locations in Cincinnati, New York, Los Angeles, and Jerusalem.

HEDER. (Hebrew for, literally, "a room.") Has come to mean a modest schoolroom where Jewish studies are taught to children. Modern all-day and afternoon religious schools have supplanted the original concept.

HEFKER. Defined as ownerless property, it is the property, according to Jewish religious law, of the first person to find it. The term has also come to mean a state of anarchy or lawlessness.

HEREM. (Hebrew for "excommunication.") Biblical injunction, rarely invoked, in which an individual Jew is formally cut off from the Jewish community for having committed a heinous sin. Rabbi Gershom, in the 11th century, issued an edict threatening excommunication to those Jews in the Ashkenazic (central and eastern Europe) community who continued to practice polygamy. Another famous case was that of Baruch Spinoza, who was excommunicated in the 17th century by the Amsterdam Jewish community.

HERETIC. Talmudic designation of those who denied the existence of God, or those who worshiped several gods or believed in the divinity of stars, planets, etc. *See also* Apikoros.

HESHVAN. Second month of the Jewish calendar. Sometimes referred to as Marheshvan—bitter Heshvan, because no Jewish holidays occur in that month.

HEVRAH KADDISHAH. (Hebrew and Aramaic for "holy brotherhood.") Volunteer group devoted to providing ritual burial for the Jewish dead in the community and offering comfort to the mourning family. With the advent of modern funeral parlors such groups have diminished in importance.

HILLEL. Rabbinic and academic leader whose interpretations of religious law and practice are usually considered more lenient and flexible than those of his colleague, the severe Shammai. Devoted to Torah study, he cautioned his Rabbinic colleagues against getting involved in the politics of the day (1st century B.C.E.). Hillel foundations honoring him are centers of Jewish study and activity on many college campuses.

HILLUL HASHEM. (Hebrew for "desecration of the name.") Any deliberate violation of a Jewish law is considered an act of desecration that detracts from the glory of God. Thus any disreputable act on the part of a Jew—particularly against a non-Jew—is regarded as a *Hillul Hashem.*

HOL HAMOED. Intermediate days of a festival, e.g., those between the first and last days of Passover, and those between the first and last days of the Sukkoth holiday. Religious services on those days are partly holiday and partly daily in form. Some Jews do not use the phylacteries (see Tefillin) on Hol Hamoed, while others do but refrain from reciting a blessing. (Phylacteries are not put on on Sabbath and festivals.)

HOLY ARK. (*Aron kodesh* in Hebrew.) Synagogue ark in which the Torah scrolls are kept. Opened only to remove or return the scrolls, or during special services. A curtain known as a parochet, usually made of velvet and embroidered with traditional ornamental symbols, covers the ark when it is not in use. The ark is generally on a raised platform, often the same platform from which the Rabbi leads the service.

HOLY CITY. Traditional designation of Jerusalem. Three cities have traditionally been revered as sacred, in addition to Jerusalem: Hebron, Tiberias, and Safed.

HOLY LAND. The appellation traces back to a Biblical reference and is repeated in Talmudic passages. In Jewish law certain commandments could be fulfilled only in the Holy Land. During the nearly two millennia of the Diaspora it was customary for Jews who had died to be buried in their native lands with a bit of soil brought over long distances from the Holy Land.

HOLY SCRIPTURES. *See* Bible.

HOLY TEMPLE. The First Temple was built by King Solomon on Mount Moriah in Jerusalem and destroyed in 587 B.C.E. by Nebuchadnezzar. The Second Temple was begun by permission of Cyrus in 538 B.C.E., and remained the chief religious edifice of the Jews until 70 C.E., when it was destroyed by the Romans, led by Titus. (The 9th of Av, Tisha B'Av, remains to this day a mourning and fast day in

Torah breastplate of silver with cast
ornaments. Augsburg, 1813.

memory of the Holy Temple.) The site of the Temple has been occupied by the Mosque of Omar, erected in the 8th century.

HOLY TONGUE. Hebrew, by virtue of the fact that the Bible and most of the literary treasures of the Jews were composed in that language, is considered sacred. Throughout the Diaspora, Hebrew was reserved for study and prayer and was not used in daily life. Some ultra-Orthodox groups still refuse to speak Hebrew, considering it too sacred for daily usage. They generally use Yiddish as their daily language.

HOSHANAH RABBAH. Seventh day of Sukkoth. In Temple days worshippers walked around the altar of the Temple seven times, explaining *"Hoshanah"* ("O, deliver us") and waving the *lulav* and *etrog.* Seven circuits of the synagogue are made today on Hoshanah Rabbah. The day is also popularly looked upon as the final day of judgment, culminating three weeks of penitence that began on Rosh Hashanah.

HOSHANOT. Liturgical poems, including selections from Psalms, recited during the Hoshanah Rabbah circuit of the synagogue.

HOSHEN. Breastplate used in antiquity by the High Priest, and used today as a decoration for the scroll of the Law, and resembling the ancient symbol. *See also* Torah Ornaments.

HOSPITALITY. (*Hachnassat orchim* in Hebrew.) The practice of hospitality, a strongly entrenched concept in Jewish life, is traced to Abraham, who opened his home (according to legend) to all, including idolators, in the hope that they would be brought closer to belief in God. The opening words of the Passover seder service read: "All who are hungry, come and eat." In most European communities, until about a half century ago, impoverished students and travelers could count on a Sabbath meal at the very least at the table of hosts practicing the concept of hospitality.

HUMASH. Any of the Five Books of Moses is called a humash (literally, "a fifth").

HUMILITY. The Rabbis listed humility as the greatest of Jewish virtues, pointing to Moses, who is described in the Bible as "exceedingly humble, above all the men that were upon the face of the earth." Micah's famous phrase "And what doth the Lord require of thee but to do justly, to love mercy, and to walk humbly with thy God" is characterized in the Talmud as containing all the teachings of the Torah.

HUPPAH. Today the word refers to the canopy held above the bride and groom during a Jewish wedding ceremony. In ancient times it referred to the bridal chamber where the marriage was consummated.

I

IDOLATRY. Worship of gods, statues, images, the sun, moon, stars, etc., is strongly condemned in Jewish religious law. The three gravest sins in Judaism are murder, sexual immorality, and idolatry.

ILLEGITIMACY. Jewish law distinguishes between the *mamzer* (usually translated as "bastard") and other types of illegitimate children. A *mamzer* is a child born of an incestuous union or as the result of a married woman having had relations with a man other than her husband. Such children are permitted to marry one another but not within the regular Jewish community. Foundlings or the children of unmarried women are treated far more leniently, and efforts are generally made to legitimize their status.

ILLUI. An outstanding, brilliant student, usually a young Talmudist.

IM YIRTZE HASHEM. Frequently used expression by religious Jews that translates as "If God [the Name] wills it."

IMMERSION. Ritual purification (called tevilah) for a religious purpose. Immersion can take place in a mikveh (a ritual bath), a requirement of converts to Judaism; Orthodox women immerse themselves after menstruation. Utensils that have become ritually unfit may also be immersed and made ready for use.

IMMORTALITY. This concept is not included in the Bible or in early Rabbinic writings. However, over the centuries there has emerged a concept of immortality of the soul—an idea that is generally, if passively, accepted by most Jews and religious thinkers.

INDEPENDENCE DAY. Israel's founding in 1948, celebrated on the 5th day of Iyar, has become a part holiday among most Jews. Mourning regulations are waived and the half hallel is included in the morning service. The celebration is known as Yom Haatzmauth.

INITIALS. The practice of using initials to refer to certain terms is ancient in Judaism; e.g., the Rambam means Rabbi Moshe Ben Maimon, or Maimonides.

INSULT. In Jewish law, an insult is likened to an injury, and is to be compensated. The Talmud teaches that he who "insults his fellow in public has no share in the world to come."

INTERMARRIAGE. Marriage between a Jew and a non-Jew is prohibited. Such a marriage is not looked upon as valid and therefore requires no formal divorce to be dissolved. A child from such a union is considered Jewish if the mother is Jewish. If the non-Jewish partner has converted to Judaism, the marriage is regarded as fully valid.

INVOCATION. Brief prayer usually offered by a Rabbi at a public meeting, asking God's blessing on the group's endeavor. Not practiced in Israel.

ISRAEL. Traditional name—Eretz Israel ("Land of Israel")—for the land that God promised Abraham and his seed. The land is regarded as God's gift to the Jewish people, and as part of the covenant. Religious tradition states that it is possible to abide by the Torah laws more fully in Israel than anywhere else. The traditional Jewish prayer book is Israel-oriented, and includes special references to Israel's seasonal needs for rain and dew. According to the Talmud, prophecy can only take place in Israel. About 22 percent of the world's Jews live in Israel today.

ISRAELITE. Usually refers to the Jews of Bible times. Jews are divided into three religious categories: the Kohanim, or members of the priestly tribe; the Levites, descendants of those who aided the priests; and the Israelites, including the bulk of Jews. When congregants are called to the reading of the Torah in synagogue, the first section is accorded to the Kohanim, the second to the Levites, and the remaining portions to the Israelites.

IYAR. Eighth month of the Jewish religious calendar in which Israel Independence Day falls.

J

JEW. Anglicized version of the Hebrew word *yehudi*, literally a member of the tribe of Judah. A Jew is one born to a Jewish mother, or a convert to Judaism. Converts have exactly the same rights as all other Jews with one exception—a female convert may not marry a Kohen, a member of the priestly group.

JEWISH SCIENCE. Small Jewish religious group, established in 1924 in the U.S. by Rabbi Morris Lichtenstein. The group's teachings stress the spiritual rather than ritual side of the Jewish religion, and take an essentially optimistic view of life.

JEWISH THEOLOGICAL SEMINARY. Fountainhead of the Conservative wing of Judaism in the U.S. Various educational, cultural, religious, and other organizations are affiliated with it. It has branches in Los Angeles and Jerusalem, and owns one of the world's finest collections of Judaica. Although it was begun in the latter part of the 19th century, the seminary was reorganized in 1902 and dates its growth from that year.

JORDAN. Largest river in Israel. The Jordan flows from the foothills of Mount Hermon to the Dead Sea, the lowest spot on earth. The river is mentioned in the Bible and figures in post-Biblical times as a site for ascetic sects, including the Essenes.

JOURNEY. A special prayer for a forthcoming journey (minimum distance, three miles) is recited by the observant. Travelers on Israel airliners are handed a printed copy of the prayer upon boarding.

JOY. Worship with joyfulness is a basic Jewish tenet. The Rabbis wrote that "the divine presence does not rest upon a man while he is in a state of gloom, but only through the joy with which he fulfills his commandments." Family celebrations such as a circumcision, bar or bat mitzvah, or of course a wedding are occasions for exultant manifestations of joy. The followers of the Hasidic movement have concentrated on making joyous enthusiasm a major part of their worship.

JUBILEE. Biblical law stipulated a Jubilee was to take place every 50th year, when all slaves were to be freed, while all lands (except those inherited) were to revert to their original owners. With the Temple's destruction, the Jubilee was abandoned, but tradition states it is to be reinstated when all Jews live in Israel again.

JUDAH THE MACCABEE. Eldest son of Mattathias, who in true guerrilla style led his military bands against the conquerors of Israel (in the 2d century B.C.E.), eventually liberating Jerusalem and rededicating the profaned Temple. *See also* Hanukkah.

JUDAISM. The Jewish religion, or as interpreted by some the totality of Jewish mores, tenets, values, and attitudes. Judaism is based on monotheism and stresses ethical behavior. The ethical teachings of the Prophets and the legal-ritual precepts formulated by the priests meshed in the codes developed by the early Rabbis. Although there are 613 commandments a Jew should observe including many associated with the Temple service, there is also a philosophical-intellectual interpretation of Judaism that may be said to be constantly undergoing change. The question, Who is a Jew? has been raised through the centuries, and the answers have never been wholly satisfactory to all. Judaism does not have a binding, formal credo, although Maimonides wrote the "13 Articles of Faith," which many Jews have to a greater or lesser degree accepted as their understanding of their faith.

JUDGE. There were judges appointed by Moses even before the Israelites entered the promised land. During the time of the Second Temple there was a Sanhedrin comprised of 71 judges. The position withered after the destruction of the Temple and the subsequent exile, but many Rabbis took on judicial roles. In any but a minor case there was a body of three judges—often but not always three Rabbis—constituted as a Bet Din. Such tribunals, interpreting religious law when the parties agreed beforehand to abide by the court's rulings, function today in the U.S.

JUSTICE. The Rabbis interpreted the meting out of justice as requiring tempering with mercy. However, they taught that mercy cannot deflect true justice but can only modify the final verdict.

KABBALAH. (Hebrew for "tradition, or receiving.") Overall designation for Jewish mysticism. Before the 13th century the term referred only to the writings of the Prophets and the oral law, but since then it has come to mean mysticism. Kabbalists looked at divinity as a pure, infinite, spiritual light, whose emanations account for all creation. They also held that man's soul was formed in the "upper spheres" and that the goal of the soul is to come closer to the divine source. Jewish mystics believed that it was incumbent upon Jews to live in a state of sanctity, brotherhood, and unity. They believed that mystical doctrines were given to Moses on Mount Sinai and are hidden in the Torah and the oral law. The movement flourished in the 15th and 16th centuries, and was centered in the mountain city of Safed in Israel. Some traces of kabbalah, particularly those dealing with magical forms, continued and to some extent influenced the Hasidic movement.

KABBALAT SHABBAT. Reception of the Sabbath. A

special service on Friday evening preceding the regular service, inaugurating the weekly day of rest. The service was initiated some 400 years ago by the kabbalists of Safed.

KADDISH. Ancient prayer, recited in Aramaic, which sanctifies the name of the Lord, and is today the mourner's prayer, recited thrice daily by a mourner for 11 months and a day, and on the yahrzeit of the decedent's anniversary. There are also special versions of the prayer declaimed by the cantor or leader of the service.

KALLAH. (Hebrew for "bride.") In another meaning entirely, kallah is a study retreat dating back to Talmudic days, when scholars met twice yearly to exchange ideas and interpretations of law. In recent years, various organizations have reorganized the kallah idea, with students meeting for the purpose of intense Jewish learning, usually over a long weekend in a rural setting.

KAPOTA. Long, often silky outer garment that originated in eastern Europe and is still worn by some Hasidic or ultra-Orthodox Jews.

KAPPAROT. (Hebrew for "expiations.") Ancient custom that has been denounced by some Rabbinic authorities as paganistic and superstitious in which Jews, on the morning of the eve of the Day of Atonement (Yom Kippur), take a fowl and swing it around the head while reciting specified verses, including: "This is my redemption, this rooster shall be killed while I shall be admitted to and allowed to live a long, happy, and peaceful life." (A man uses a cock; a female uses a hen.) Almost all people today use a sum of money instead of the fowl, and donate the sum to charity.

KARAITE. Jewish sect dating back to the 8th century that rejected the oral law. Led by Saadyah, in the 9th century, Rabbis attacked their views and blocked their development. Marriage between Jews and Karaites was forbidden, and today there are only a few thousand left, living mostly in Israel. The Karaites insist on rigid, literal interpretation of Biblical law and have no regard for post-Biblical holidays such as Hanukkah, or the use of a mezuzah or phylacteries.

KASHER. To make utensils or meat ritually pure. The word "kosher" (q.v.), meaning food prepared according to Jewish dietary laws, is known in Israel as "kasher," because of differences of pronunciation.

KASHRUT. *See* Kosher.

KEHILLAH. (Hebrew for, literally, "community.") Used to designate an organized Jewish community which was often responsible for internal affairs. Such an organization functioned for a brief time in New York.

KETER TORAH. (Hebrew for "crown of the Law.") Usually made of silver, a large regal crown with two sockets in which the tops of the rollers of the scroll of the Law are inserted. The keter symbolizes the kingship of the law.

KETUBAH. Traditional Jewish marriage contract, written in Aramaic, listing the groom's obligations to the bride. The ketubah is usually read aloud during the wedding ceremony by the officiating Rabbi after it has been signed by two witnesses not related to the prospective couple. Reform Jewish ceremonies do not usually include the ketubah in the ceremony; Conservative Jews have made some small alterations in the language. In recent years, newlyweds have taken to decorating their ketubah so that it becomes an artistic conversation piece as well as a Jewish religious-legal document.

KIDDUSH. (Hebrew for "sanctification.") Special blessing over a cup of wine, preceding the Sabbath eve or holiday eve meal, expressing a sense of the holiness of the day. Customarily the head of the household intones the blessing, sips some wine, and offers it to all present. Kiddush is also recited in the synagogue on Friday and holiday eves, on the theory that there may be some among the congregation who will not be able to recite their own blessing when they return home.

A marriage contract in ink,
tempera on parchment, 1817.

KIDDUSH HASHEM. (Hebrew for "sanctification of
the name.") Usually refers to acts of martyrdom,
when Jews, as in the days of the Spanish Inquisition,
preferred death at the stake to renouncing their faith.
In the broader sense the term denotes any worthy
action on the part of Jews that enhances the prestige
of Judaism in the eyes of non-Jews.

KIDDUSH LEVANAH. (Hebrew for "sanctification of the moon.") A special service recited in the synagogue's courtyard on the Saturday night preceding the tenth day of the new lunar month. The blessing stresses the cycle of nature's constant renewal as symbolic of the Jewish people's renewal and redemption.

KIDDUSHIN. (Hebrew for "betrothal.") Kiddushin is followed by nissuin, the consummation of the marriage.

KIDNAPPING. Biblical law asserts that he who "stealeth a man, and selleth him, or if he be found in his hand, he shall surely be put to death." Capital punishment, however, was carried out only if the kidnapper had abducted the victim, depriving him of personal liberty, had sold him as a slave to a stranger, and had treated the victim as a slave before selling him.

KINDLING OF LIGHTS. The woman of the household traditionally kindles candles on the eve of the Sabbath or holiday, signifying the approach of a day of cheerfulness and light. If a woman cannot light the candles, the obligation falls on the man of the household.

KINNOT. Special mournful prayers recited in the synagogue on Tisha B'Av.

KIPPAH. Skullcap. *See also* Yarmulke.

KISLEV. Third month in the Hebrew calendar in which Hannukah occurs.

KITTEL. Long, white outer garment generally worn at the seder table and in synagogue on Yom Kippur. In some communities, in past centuries, it was also worn by male worshippers on the Sabbath and festivals.

KLAUS. (German for "enclosure.") A study house for adults which also served as a synagogue, in which Talmudic tractates were studied. The term was first used in the 17th century and originated in central Europe. Members of Hasidic groups Yiddishized the word, calling a synagogue a *kloiz*.

KOHEN (pl. Kohanim). Member of the priestly tribe. A Kohen is accorded the honor of being called first to the reading of the Torah in synagogue. In the Orthodox tradition he may not marry a divorcee nor may he come in contact with a corpse or go to a cemetery. At the end of certain prayer services the Kohanim bless the congregation.

KOL NIDRE. (Aramaic for "all vows.") The mournful prayer that opens the Yom Kippur eve service, in which the worshiper declares that all vows made unwittingly or rashly shall be nullified. The congregation stands up for this prayer, the holy ark is opened, two scrolls of the Law are placed on either side of the cantor, and the recitation takes place, chanted to a melody that is said to be more than 1000 years old. Anti-Semitic comments notwithstanding, the vows

The Western Wall.

refer only to those made between man and God—
other vows can only be annulled by mutual consent.

KOSHER. (Hebrew for, literally, "pure.") Refers to
foods permissible under Jewish dietary laws. The
term "kashrut" refers to the dietary laws system.
Symbols of kosher foods used in the U.S. include the
letters OK, and a U enclosed in an O.

KOTEL. (Hebrew for "wall.") Refers to the Western
Wall, the only remaining section of the Holy Temple
still standing in Jerusalem. It was reincorporated
into Israel after the 1967 Six-Day War. Services are
held daily at the Wall, and in recent years the custom
of having a bar mitzvah boy read his Biblical portion
at the site has grown.

L

LABOR. Judaism takes a positive attitude toward
labor, citing the Biblical phrase "six days shalt thou
work," which precedes the phrase "and on the
seventh day shalt thou rest." Talmudic references
to labor include: "Great is labor for it lends dignity
to man"; "Idleness leads to immorality and degenera-
tion"; and "He who does not teach his son a trade,
teaches him brigandage." The Bible commanded that
a day laborer was to be paid promptly at the end of
his day's work.

LAG B'OMER. Minor festival that falls between Passover and Shavuoth. Commemorates the end of a
plague that killed many students of Rabbi Akiba.
Rabbi Simeon bar Yochai, allegedly the author of the
Zohar, the central work of Jewish mysticism, is also
said to have died on Lag B'Omer (the 18th day of
Iyar). In tribute to him, some Hasidic and other Jews
journey to Meron, the purported burial place of Rabbi
Simeon, give their young sons their first haircuts
on the spot, and sing and dance around bonfires
through the night.

LAMED VAV. In numerology, the two Hebrew letters
lamed and vav add up to 36—according to an ancient
Jewish tradition, the world continues to exist because

of the righteousness of 36 people. A person so described by others is therefore a truly saintly soul. Such people are called lamedvavniks.

LAW. Jewish religious law is usually called the Halachah, while the Torah (the Pentateuch) is described as the Law, with a capital L. A separate part of the law is called the "oral law" (*Torah sheb'al peh*)—that part of the law revealed to Moses but not recorded. Thus in Rabbinic thinking Jewish law is comprised both of the written and the oral laws, as recorded in the Torah and the Talmud.

LESHANA HABAA B'YERUSHALAYIM. (Hebrew for "next year in Jerusalem.") Phrase that concludes the seder service on Passover, denoting the deep attachment of the Jewish people to the Holy City through the centuries of their dispersion. Israelis who live in cities other than Jerusalem have changed the phrase to read *"Leshana Habaa B'Yerushalayim Habnuyah"* ("Next year, in rebuilt Jerusalem").

LESHANA TOVAH TIKATEVU. (Hebrew for "May you be inscribed for a good year.") Traditional greeting among Jews on the occasion of Rosh Hashanah, the Jewish New Year. Tradition teaches that on Rosh Hashanah God writes the fate of all people, and seals the decision on Yom Kippur. Hence the ten days between these two Holy Days are known as the ten days of awe or ten days of penitence.

LESHON HA-RA. (Hebrew for "tongue of evil.") Slander spreaders or tale-bearers are sharply condemned in the Bible and in the Rabbinic writings. Some Rabbis went so far as to say that talebearing was even more sinful than the cardinal sins of murder, immorality, and idolatry. The prohibitions against spreading rumors about others were equally severe against the talebearer and the person willing to listen.

LEVAYAH. Funeral procession. Literally, accompanying the decedent to his last resting place.

LEVIRATE MARRIAGE. Biblical injunction to marry the widow of a brother who has died without having fathered any children. Therefore, a ceremony called halitzah enables the deceased's brother to be freed from this obligation.

LEVITES. Descendants of Levi, one of Jacob's 12 sons, who are required to help the members of the priestly tribe in their religious duties. A Levite is generally called second, after the Kohen, in being honored at the reading of the Torah.

LIFE. Judaism sees life as God's supreme blessing. The Torah is termed a tree of life. The Talmud teaches that "whoever destroys one life is as if he destroyed a whole world, and whoever preserves one life is as if he preserved a whole world." For that reason, mercy killings are forbidden. The familiar Jewish toast *"L'chayim"* means "To life."

LULAV. Palm branch. Held together with the myrtle and willow in the right hand, and the *etrog* in the left, it is blessed during the morning service of the Sukkoth festival (except on the Sabbath).

MAARIV. Evening service, recited after nightfall. It includes the shema, the amidah, and aleinu, and usually follows immediately after the minha or afternoon service.

MAASEH BOOKS. Folk tales, based on Talmudic sources, in Yiddish that began to appear in the 15th century. They always had a moral and religious message.

MAASER. Tithe. 10 percent of a person's income, which is to be set aside for a specific, i.e., charitable purpose.

MACCABEES. *See* Hasmoneans; Hanukkah.

MACHPELAH. Cave in which Sarah was buried, located near Hebron. The three Patriarchs and their wives are believed to be buried in the tomb, which has a mosque on the site. Rachel is buried in nearby Bethlehem.

MAFTIR. Final section of the Sabbath and holiday

reading of the Torah. Followed by a section from the Prophets (the haftarah). It is considered a special honor to be called to the maftir.

MAGEN DAVID. Shield of David. Two triangles of equal size, one superimposed on the other, forming a six-pointed star. It is the emblem of the Jewish people, and appears on the Israeli flag. Although found in early synagogues and cemeteries, its origin is unknown and there is no Biblical nor Talmudic reference to it. A red Magen David is the official emblem of Israel's equivalent to the Red Cross.

MAGGID. Wandering, itinerant popular preacher first

Maimonides

known in the 11th century, who confined his talks to easily understood homiletics. In some communities the Rabbi preached a formal sermon only twice yearly, leaving the local maggid the task of speaking to the people more frequently.

MAGIC. The practice of magic when associated with idolatry is expressly forbidden by the Bible, under penalty of death. Talmudic references to practitioners of sorcery refer to them in the feminine gender, implying that women were most active in this area.

MAH NISHTANAH. Opening words of the four questions asked at the seder service by the youngest child present. The reading of the Passover Haggadah is in effect a long reply to these questions.

MAHZOR. Festival prayer book as distinct from the daily prayer book. The most commonly used mahzor is the one for the High Holy Days.

MAIMONIDES. 12th-century philosopher of Judaism and codifier of Biblical and Talmudic laws. Born in Spain, he spent most of his life in Egypt where he was physician to the court. His best-known works, *Mishne Torah* and *Guide for the Perplexed*, are studied eagerly to this day.

MAOT HITTIM. (Hebrew for "wheat money.") Funds distributed to the needy on Passover eve. Although some organizations still provide the poor with matzah and wine for Passover use, most synagogues collect maot hittim gifts and distribute the money to those in need.

MAPPAH. *See* Torah Ornaments.

MAROR. Generic term used for any bitter vegetable eaten during the seder to commemorate the Israelites who were slaves in Egypt and whose lives were "embittered" until the liberation and exodus. During the seder ceremony, the maror is eaten twice—once with the haroset and once with matzah.

MARRANOS. Secret Jews in the Iberian peninsula who, under pressure from the Inquisition in the 14th and 15th centuries, lived overtly as practicing Catholics, but covertly followed the customs and rules of their religion. Most Marranos reemerged as Jews when they escaped to other countries, but some remained on, their Jewish observances dwindling with the passage of time. A few small groups in Spain still observe rites that indicate they are descended from the Marranos.

MASHGIAH. Religious supervisor, generally employed by a hotel, restaurant, or caterer to ascertain that all food served is in strict accordance with Jewish dietary laws.

MATRIARCHS. Sarah, Rebecca, Leah, and Rachel, the wives of the Patriarchs. Tradition teaches that they were endowed with outstanding qualities, including modesty and virtuousness.

MATRIMONY. Judaism looks upon the matrimonial state as socially, morally, and religiously ideal and as a prerequisite to spiritual fulfillment. Celibacy is frowned on, with the Rabbis stating that he "who dwells without a wife dwells without joy, without blessing, without good, and without happiness." Marriage is looked upon as a religious duty, with the purpose of procreation clearly spelled out. After ten years of childlessness, a husband has the right to sue for divorce although this is practically never done nowadays.

MATZAH. Unleavened bread, the only kind that may be eaten during the Passover holiday, is a reminder of the Israelites' swift flight from the Egyptians— they did not have time for the dough to rise as they raced toward freedom.

MATZAH SHMURAH. Specially "guarded" matzah, prepared by the very observant for Passover. The flour for this matzah is supervised from the time the wheat is harvested until it is baked, to ensure it does not contact any fermenting agent or moisture.

MATZEVAH. (Hebrew for, literally, "raised stone.") Monument erected at a grave site.

MAZAL TOV. (Hebrew for "Good luck.") Congratulatory phrase. Among some eastern Jews a handshake

Torah mantle of silk brocade
embroidered with silver thread. Holland, 1787.

and the expression *"Mazal bracha"* ("Luck and a blessing") often signify the closing of a business deal.

MEGILLAH. (Hebrew for "scroll.") All early written works were in the forms of scrolls written on parchment. The best-known megillah included in the Bible is the Book of Esther, recounting the Purim story. On Purim eve, the synagogue is packed with children waiting for the name Haman to be read aloud, at which point they stomp their feet and wave their groggers.

MEHITZA. Partition used in Orthodox synagogues separating men and women during public prayers.

ME'IL. Ornamental, brocaded mantle that covers the scroll of the Law.

MELAMED. Teacher, usually of young children. In the Yiddish vernacular, a melamed has a pejorative connotation—one who has not risen above being a teacher of small children.

Austrian menorah, c. 1870.

MELAVEH MALKA. Festive meal, often accompanied by singing, "accompanying the Queen Sabbath" on her way, held at the end of the Sabbath.

MENORAH. Seven-branched candelabrum described

North African menorah, 18th-century.

in the Bible and used in Temple days. Today it is the official emblem of Israel. Most synagogues utilize a menorah as part of the decor in the sanctuary. The special menorah for Hanukkah has eight candlesticks and a ninth for the shammash (server). To distinguish the two, the latter is called a Hanukkiyah.

METIVTA. Rabbinic school, generally for more advanced students.

MEZUZAH. (Hebrew for "doorpost.") Small piece of parchment on which are inscribed the first two verses of the shema prayer, tightly rolled and placed inside a small case with an opening through which the single word *Shadai* ("Almighty") may be seen. The mezuzah is affixed to the right doorpost of a Jew's

Middle Eastern mezuzah, 20th century.

home, in accordance with Biblical injunction. Some Jews touch the mezuzah on entering and leaving, and then lightly kiss their fingers. Small versions of the mezuzah are now worn by some men and women as a good-luck charm or as a display of their commitment to Judaism.

MI SHEBERACH. First words of a special prayer offered in synagogue for the recovery of a member (or a congregant's relative or friend) who is acutely ill.

MIDRASH. Discovery of meanings in the Bible other than the literal interpretation. (The word root *darash* means "to inquire" or "to investigate.") The practice was instituted in order to better understand specific Biblical commands or prohibitions. It took many scholars and considerable time to spell out, for example, which kinds of labor were prohibited on the Sabbath.

MIDRASHIC LITERATURE. While the Halachah-oriented Midrash sought to extract the laws from the Biblical text, the Aggadah-oriented Midrash searched for ethical and moral connotations.

MIKVEH. Ritual bath in which women immerse themselves after menstruation. *See also* Immersion.

MINHA. Afternoon daily service which may be recited after noon and before sunset. It is usually combined with the maariv or evening service.

MINHAG. (Hebrew for "custom.") Religious custom that has been generally accepted and that takes on the force of Mosaic law.

MINYAN. Quorum of ten males over the age of 13. Required for a congregational service. Although it is permissible to pray alone, it is not permitted to recite certain prayers, such as kaddish, the mourner's prayer, without a minyan. Some Jewish feminists have been pressing for inclusion in a minyan, and in some congregations (not Orthodox) their demands have been met.

MISHLOACH MANOT. Exchanging food, gifts, dating back to ancient times, was instituted to provide for the needy. At Purim, friends and neighbors often send one another small tokens.

MISHNAH. *See* Talmud.

MITNAGDIM. Opponents of the Hasidic movement. Originally the Mitnagdim objected to the Hasidic followers making light of study and concentrating on vociferous singing and shouting during services. With the onset of the secular age the bitter rivalry between the groups subsided.

MITZVAH. Divine commandment. The mitzvot are divided between those between man and God, and those between man and man. The Torah lists a total of 613 injunctions—365 "do nots" and 248 "dos." There are also numerous commands of post-Biblical origin. The word today is also loosely translated as "a good deed."

MIZRACH. (Hebrew for "east.") The Jews pray toward the east, toward Jerusalem. The eastern wall of the synagogue, where the holy ark is placed, is therefore an honored place for worshipers. Thus mizrach refers to the eastern wall of the synagogue. In addition, there are wall plaques hung in the home with the word "mizrach" prominently adorned.

MOADIM L'SIMCHA. Expression of greeting on festival days, meaning "May you have festivals for rejoicing." Another such phrase is *"Hag same-ach"* ("Happy holiday"); *"Gut yontiff,"* of Yiddish origin, is also still in vogue.

MOHEL. Person trained and authorized to perform a circumcision. A mohel is generally highly regarded in the community.

MONOTHEISM. Fundamental precept of Judaism, which sees God as absolutely above nature and in full control of natural forces. Jewish sources teach that God was not born nor does he beget other divinities. He is omnipotent, and is independent of matter or other beings. At the same time, he enters into a direct, personal relationship with his creatures and is concerned with their well-being. Abraham is generally considered to have enunciated the first concept of monotheism.

MONTH, BLESSING OF. Special addition to the Sabbath service preceding the new month when a prayer is offered for the congregation's welfare. It is omitted for Tishri, when Rosh Hashanah commences.

MOTHER. Although the Bible asserts that the father "takes precedence over the mother in all matters," the equal rights of both parents in ethical affairs are stressed in Jewish teaching. The Matriarchs are as highly regarded in Judaism as are the Patriarchs. Home and family life are centered around the mother, whose responsibility for transmitting the Jewish ethical values is traditional in Judaism.

MOTZI. Key word in the special blessing on bread, signifying the individual's thanks for having ample food to eat. At most public Jewish functions, including private weddings and bar and bat mitzvah celebrations, the honor of leading the group in recitation of the blessing is reserved for the Rabbi or a grandparent.

MOURNING. Rules of behavior by a mourner date to Biblical times. While warning against excessive mourning, Judaism seems to teach that openly proclaiming one's desolation at the loss of a loved one is a healthy, normal act, which will in time be replaced by a positive attitude to life. Thus a mourner (for immediate family) sits shivah (seven days) at home, on a low bench, unshaven, the mirrors covered, no radio or television turned on, reciting the kaddish prayer thrice daily—but at the same time it is incumbent on friends to visit him, to chat about the deceased and about trivia, to help bridge the first shock of his loss. After 30 days the mourner may shave, but must refrain from visiting places of amusement for a full year. He continues to visit the synagogue daily, recites the prayers in unison with other members of the congregation, and somehow the sense of continuity and of life being worthwhile takes hold.

MUKTZEH. Objects that are forbidden to be touched on the Sabbath, e.g., tools and money.

MUSAF. Additional service recited on the mornings of Sabbath, festivals, and the first day of the new month.

NAME. Religiously, Jews are known by their own names and those of their fathers. Thus, when one is called to the reading of the Torah, or becomes bar mitzvah, the family name is omitted but the person called will be summoned, for example, as "Abraham, son of Jacob." The names of Abram, Sarai, and Jacob were changed to Abraham, Sarah, and Israel when they entered a new plane of life. A male who is critically ill often has the name Chayim ("life") added to his own; Chaya is the name given to a woman.

NASI. Loosely translated as "prince," the title was given to political leaders of the Jews in certain parts of the Roman Empire. The lay leader of a Jewish community, in later generations, was also accorded this special appellation. In Israel, the president of the state is still known as the nasi.

NAZIRITE. Person who vows to live an ascetic life, including abstention from drinking wine or cutting his hair or being in contact with a corpse. A Nazirite can undertake such an existence for a brief span of time or forever, in which case he could thin his hair annually. Samson was a Nazirite. Women could also undertake to become Nazirites. Although the Rabbis did not encourage such a step, they recognized that in certain cases it was necessary for individuals who wished to break with their past and start life anew.

NEDAVAH. In Biblical times a free-will offering. Today translated as a donation to a worthy cause.

NEILAH. (Hebrew for "closing.") Final section of the virtually all-day Yom Kippur service, signifying that the gates of heaven are closed, and the worshiper's fate has been sealed for the forthcoming year. The congregation remains standing through the service, the holy ark is opened, and the closing sound heard is the blasting of the shofar, followed by the congregants' response, "Next year in Jerusalem." Neilah always coincides with the setting of the sun.

NER TAMID. Eternal light seen hanging above the holy ark in every synagogue; it recalls the Biblical injunction for a continually burning light in the Holy Temple.

NETUREI KARTA. (Aramaic for "guardians of the city.") Small group of Orthodox extremists, concentrated in Jerusalem, who refuse to recognize the legitimacy of Israel. In their view, only the Messiah's advent will ensure the establishment of a theocracy, which they support.

NEVIIM. (Hebrew for "Prophets.") The second section of three in the Bible. The first is the Torah, also known as the Pentateuch or Five Books of Moses; Prophets, the second section, includes Isaiah, Jeremiah, etc.; the third part, known as Ketuvim or Holy Writings, includes Psalms, Proverbs, Ruth, Esther, Song of Songs.

NIDAH. Menstruating woman. She is not allowed to have relations with her husband until 12 days after the end of her discharge, and only after immersion in a mikveh.

NIGGUN. Traditional chant to a prayer. Among the Hasidic adherents, the singing of a wordless niggun is often a highlight of a gathering.

NINE DAYS. Nine days from the 1st to the 9th of Av are a mourning period during which Orthodox Jews refrain from eating meat or drinking wine. The period coincides with the final seige of Jerusalem that culminated in the destruction of the Holy Temple on Tisha B'Av (the 9th of Av).

NISAN. Seventh month of the Jewish religious calendar.

NOACHIAN LAWS. Traditionally, the injunctions handed to Noah, who was not Jewish (Abraham is considered to have been the first Jew). They are therefore obligatory for all people. The Talmud explains that the seven Noachian Laws are derived from the

Silver Sabbath lamp in the form of the
fountain of life. Frankfurt, c. 1710.

early chapters of Genesis—the administration of Justice, and prohibitions against blasphemy, idolatry, sexual immorality, murder, robbery, and eating part of a living animal.

NUMBERS. System of numbers using the Hebrew letters (aleph is 1, yod is 10, tav is 400, etc.) is called gematriah (q.v.). Mystics used various Biblical phrases numerically to arrive at interpretations or prognostications that were interesting, but little more. A Jewish calendar may be seen with the Hebrew letters tav, shin, lamed, zayin (pronounced tashlaz), which according to the gematriah system add up to 5737. Traditionally, the world was created 5737 years ago.

NUSACH. Rite or custom of prayer or service. Many prayer books are shown as following the Ashkenaz (central European) or Sepharad (Iberian) nusach.

O

OLAM HAZEH, OLAM HABA. (Hebrew for "this world, next world.") "This world" is the world around us. The phrase advises Jews to enjoy this world and not put off the pursuit of happiness to *olam haba*—the next world. *Olam haba* also refers to a Messianic age that will exist here on earth. This world, in Jewish tradition, is seen as a place where good deeds must be performed so as to store up credits for life in the next world.

OLD AGE. The Bible expressly commands people to "rise up before the hoary head and honor the face of the old man," while the Psalmist prayed: "Cast me not off in the time of old age, forsake me not when my strength faileth." By and large, the Jewish community has always been exemplary in caring for its aged population.

OLD TESTAMENT. Christian term for the Jewish Bible. The Old and New Testaments combine to form the Christian Bible. Jews often call the Jewish Bible the Holy Scriptures.

OMER. First sheaf of barley harvested. It was brought to the Temple on the second day of Passover—from this day until the holiday of Shavuoth, the counting of the omer prayer is included in daily services. The period lasts seven weeks. In the 2d century a plague erupted among Rabbi Akiva's students, and for that reason this seven-week period is a time of semi-mourning, when marriages may not take place (except on Lag B'Omer, Israel Independence Day, and on the first days of the new month). Some Orthodox Jews do not shave or cut their hair during this period.

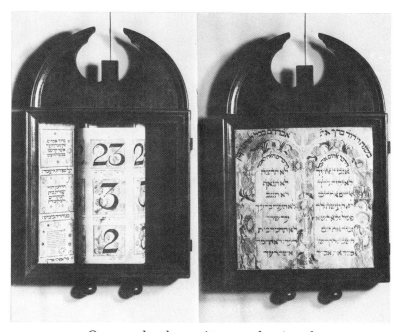

Omer calendar written and painted
on parchment. Western Europe, c. 1748.

ONEG SHABBAT. (Hebrew for "Sabbath delight.") The phrase "thou shalt call the Sabbath a delight" appears in Isaiah, and ever since, Jews have gone out of their way to transform the day of rest into a day of joyousness. In eastern Europe a century or so ago, when many Jews led impoverished lives in the rural shtetl, they somehow managed to transform their homes and lives on the Sabbath into a day of physical, mental, and spiritual respite and rejoicing. Nowadays many synagogues as well as organizations convening over a weekend will set aside a few hours on Friday evening or Saturday afternoon for an oneg shabbat—consisting of talk, singing, and refreshments.

ORGAN. Although during Temple days prayer was accompanied by instrumental music, no music accompaniment was used in synagogues virtually through the past 2000 years of dispersion. Organ music was introduced into Reform temples in Germany in the 19th century, and is today an established feature of most Reform and some Conservative houses of worship.

ORPHANS. Both the Bible and Talmudic literature emphasized the need to care for orphaned children. As the Psalmist put it, "God himself is the father of orphans." The Talmud teaches that orphans are to be spoken to softly, and their possessions protected. Whoever brings up an orphan, the Talmud says, is regarded as his father.

ORTHODOX. One of the three major wings of Judaism in the U.S., Orthodox Judaism follows most strictly the full tenets and regulations of the Halachah, Jewish religious law. Although the Orthodox wing of Judaism was by far the strongest in pre-World War I Europe, it met with severe problems when Jewish immigrants arrived in the U.S. and adopted quickly to a secular way of life. For many years, while the Conservative and Reform wings in the U.S. grew, as did the Reconstructionist movement, Orthodoxy was on the wane. However, in the past decade there has been a decided reversal, and Orthodox Jewish schools, synagogues, and groups are expanding in numbers and influence. Most Orthodox Jews would prefer not to be so designated, since they maintain that their interpretation of Judaism is the only valid one, with all other Jewish religious groups described as deviating from the mainstream of the Jewish experience. There are approximately 1 million Jewish families enrolled in Reform temples and slightly more than that in Conservative synagogues in the U.S. and Canada, but it is difficult to determine the exact number of Orthodox Jews, with figures ranging from 500,000 to over 2,500,000. One reason is because Orthodox synagogues tend to be small and numerous, compared to the fewer, larger temples and synagogues of the others. In Israel the Orthodox Rabbinate dominates the country's religious life, much to the chagrin of the fledgling Conservative and Reform groups there.

P

PARASHA. *See* Sidrah.

PARENTS. Respect for parents is a fundamental Jewish tenet, as expressed in the Decalogue. The Rabbis say parents may be disobeyed if they order their children to transgress against the Torah. Also, a son or daughter may ignore their parents' wishes when selecting a spouse but this is all. The parents are considered equal insofar as a child's duties to them is concerned.

PARNAS. (Hebrew for "provider.") A leader or a guide of the community was called a parnas, a term that is now restricted to the elders or board members of a congregation.

PAROCHET. Decorated curtain that hangs before the holy ark in the synagogue. The same term was used in Temple days to describe the partition between the holy of holies and the remainder of the Temple sanctuary. In Sephardic synagogues there is no parochet, except on Tisha B'Av, when a black mourning curtain is installed. A parochet may be of almost any color, but most synagogues hang a white curtain during the High Holy Days and on Hoshanah Rabbah.

PASCHAL SACRIFICE. Lamb that was slaughtered by the Israelites on the eve of the exodus. Its blood was sprinkled on their doorposts to ward off the angel of death. Members of the Samaritan sect sacrifice a Paschal lamb on Mount Gerizim, the group's holy site, to this day.

The oldest parochet in Prague, embroidered in 1592.

PARVE. Yiddish term denoting that a particular food is neither "dairy" nor "meat" and may be eaten at all times, e.g., fruits and vegetables.

PASSOVER. First of the three pilgrim festivals described in the Bible, beginning on the 15th day of Nisan. It lasts for eight days in the Diaspora, but only seven days in Israel. (Reform Jews also celebrate only seven days.) Known as the festival of freedom, Passover commemorates the exodus of the Israelites from Egyptian bondage. The high point of the holiday is

A word panel with illustrations of a
Passover table from the *Joel ben Simeon
Haggadah*, mid-15th century.

the family seder, observed on the first and second
nights outside Israel, and only on the first night in
Israel and by Reform Jews. Traditionally, the period
before Passover is a time of thorough housecleaning,
changing of eating and cooking utensils, and the consumption of matzah and other holiday foods during
the holiday. Passover in ancient times was also the
time of the early spring harvest.

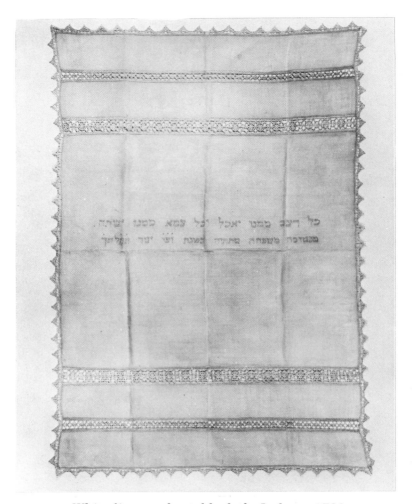

White linen seder tablecloth. Italy, c. 1760.

PASSOVER DISH. The kearah is a special seder plate on which are placed the various symbolic foods (haroset, maror, etc.) used in the service.

PATRIARCHS. Founding fathers of the Jewish people —Abraham, Isaac, and Jacob. Tradition says that the daily morning prayer was inaugurated by Abraham, the afternoon prayer by Isaac, and the evening service by Jacob.

PEACE. Peace, i.e., the absence of war, was an ideal state foreseen by Isaiah in his famous messianic

Traditional seder plate.
Central Europe,
19th century.

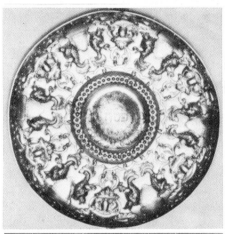

Silver seder plate.
Bologna, c. 1860.

Ceramic seder plate.
England, 1788.

vision, "Nation shall not lift up sword against nation, neither shall they know war any more." Every prayer in the Jewish liturgy contains a hope for universal peace. The daily greeting in modern Israel, "Shalom" (used both for hello and goodbye), means peace.

PEAH (pl. peot). Some Orthodox Jews, in accordance with Biblical law, allow their peot or sideburns to grow long (the Bible forbids removal of hair from the corners of the head). In ancient times the word also referred to the corners of the fields where gleanings were to be left for the poor.

PENITENCE, TEN DAYS OF. The period between Rosh Hashanah and Yom Kippur is solemn but not mournful: Jews are enjoined to concentrate on prayer, repentance, soul searching, and—on Yom Kippur— fasting. In the weeks before Rosh Hashanah, as well as during the ten days of penitence, it is customary for Jews to visit the graves of their loved ones, to pay their respects, and in a sense to ask the departed to intercede with the Almighty for them.

PEREK. *Pirkei Avoth* ("The Ethics of the Fathers"), a collection of maxims and moral teachings taken from the Talmud that is usually studied on Sabbath afternoons during the long summer months.

PHARISEES. Ancient Jewish sect described as having been especially skillful in interpreting the Torah and in adherence to the oral law. Today scholars believe that the Pharisees followed the teachings of the scholars of the time, while the Sadducees adhered to the teachings of the priests. The Pharisees' influence is felt throughout Rabbinic literature of subsequent generations.

PHYLACTERIES. *See* Tefillin.

PIKUACH NEFESH. (Hebrew for "saving of life.") Saving life takes precedence over all Biblical injunctions, and overrides all prohibitions except the three cardinal sins—idolatry, immorality, and murder. A person, for example, who is ill and has been ordered to eat by his doctor but insists on fasting on Yom Kippur is regarded as having committed a sin. In

1973, when Israel was invaded by two Arab armies, even the most Orthodox Jews did not hesitate to leave their solemn Yom Kippur service to join immediately in the country's defense.

PILGRIM FESTIVALS. (*Shalosh regalim* in Hebrew.) Every male Israelite was commanded to make a pilgrimage to Jerusalem on Passover, Shavuoth, and Sukkoth. Each pilgrim had to offer a sacrifice and bring along a tithe of produce.

PILPUL. Dialectical, hair-splitting reasoning employed in the study of the Talmud.

PIRKEI AVOTH. *See* Perek.

PIYYUT. Liturgical poem incorporated in the synagogue service, composed mainly from the 5th to the 18th centuries.

POLYGAMY. Although polygamy was permitted in Bible times, monogamy was regarded as an ideal state. Hardly any Rabbis mentioned in the Talmud had more than one wife. More than 1000 years ago polygamy was outlawed among Ashkenazic Jews; it persisted until recent times among Jews living in Muslim countries, where it is still legally sanctioned. Monogamy is the law of the land in Israel and the Sephardic Rabbinate has endorsed this ruling.

POSEKIM. Codifiers, post-Talmudic Rabbinic authorities who decided matters of Jewish law that arose in their time and attempted at the same time to systematize the amorphous mass of religious laws contained in the Talmud. Maimonides' *Mishne Torah,* written in the 12th century, is the first original attempt to codify all existing Jewish law. Another famous code is the 16th-century *Shulchan Aruch* of Rabbi Joseph Karo. Orthodox Jews still regard the latter as their standard, authoritative guide to Jewish law.

POSTMORTEMS. Jewish law requires postmortem examinations of animals slaughtered for use as food, to ensure that no defects are present in the vital organs which would make the animals unfit for consumption. Human postmortems are objected to by

Rabbinic authorities, except where such actions will help save other lives. Where religious permission for an autopsy is granted, it is on condition that all parts of the body will eventually be buried with reverence.

PRAYER. Judaism views prayer as a man's petition to God, and as praise and thanksgiving to God, as well as a statement of confession and self-judgment addressed to God. Worshipers, in accordance with Rabbi Gamliel's dictum, should recite the prayers in an undertone while they are repeated aloud by the reader. Prayer services are seen in Jewish tradition as spiritually uplifting, and as bringing men closer to God. The Talmud taught that prayers should not be recited "in a spirit of sorrow or idleness, or laughter or chatter or frivolity, but with the joyousness of performing a religious act."

PREDESTINATION. Judaism finds the concept that man's life is predetermined and his ultimate fate dependent solely on the will of God alien to Jewish tradition. The Jewish view is that man can choose between good and evil, and must strive throughout his life to opt for a life of goodness.

PROSELYTE. A non-Jew who has converted to Judaism out of inner conviction and belief is called a *ger tzedek*, a righteous proselyte. Conversion entails study of the basic Jewish laws, immersion in a ritual bath, and (for the man) circumcision. Famous proselytes in Jewish history (or their descendants) include Ruth, Rabbi Akiva, Onkelos, and Rabbi Meir. Rabbis are required to discourage prospective converts from joining the Jewish community, but once a non-Jew becomes a Jew, he is entitled to the duties and privileges accorded to all Jews.

PROSTRATION. Casting oneself on the ground during a service was customary during Temple days. It was a mark of reverence to God. In Ashkenazic services, at parts of the Rosh Hashanah and Yom Kippur services only, both the Rabbi and cantor still prostrate themselves before the holy ark. It is considered an honor for a congregant to help the Rabbi and cantor back on their feet.

PROVERBS. Second book in the third section of the Bible, the Hagiographa or Holy Writings. Containing aphorisms and specific advice on human behavior, and ascribed to King Solomon, the book's underlying theme is that true wisdom follows a basic belief in and fear of God.

PSALMS. First book of the Holy Writings, in which most of the psalms are generally ascribed to King David. Comprised of poems of praise to God. Many of the Psalms have been incorporated into the prayer book. Many older people recite them as a form of private prayer of supplication.

PSEUDEPIGRAPHA. *See* Apocrypha.

PULPIT. In ancient times a migdal was erected to facilitate the reading aloud of the Law to gatherings of Jews. The term bima ("rostrum") is more frequently used today. It is the raised platform at the front of the synagogue from which the Rabbi preaches, the cantor leads the service, and the reading of the Torah takes place.

PURIM. (Hebrew for "lots.") Occurring on the 14th day of Adar, the ancient festival marks the deliverance of the Jews in the Persian Empire from a plan by the prime minister, Haman, to commit genocide. The plan was thwarted by the intercession of Queen Esther, who revealed to King Ahasuerus that she was Jewish and that the plan was diabolical. The festival's name is taken from the casting of lots, when a given day for execution of the plan was chosen. Purim eve finds most synagogues packed, especially with youngsters who have come to hear the reading of the Book of Esther and who stomp and wave their groggers whenever Haman's name is read out. In Israel today Purim is often celebrated by masquerade balls and children's parades. At the traditional Purim seudah, or festive meal, drinking is encouraged.

PUSHKA. Small money can for charitable purposes into which the woman of the household drops a few coins before lighting the Sabbath eve candles. It is also used by other family members to collect monies for charitable purposes.

R

RABBI. (Hebrew for "my master.") Originally a title used in addressing scholars and sages in ancient times, the title is limited nowadays to individuals who have been ordained, usually by a recognized Rabbinic seminary, although ordination may also be conferred by a Rabbi or group of Rabbis. Until the Middle Ages Rabbis pursued various occupations and acted as spiritual leaders of their congregations or communities without compensation. Since that time the Rabbinate has become a full-time, paid vocation. Although a Rabbi's chief religious function is to interpret and decide matters of Jewish law, he is also called on today to be partly an educator, a counselor to his congregants, a Jewish community spokesman, a visitor to the sick and bereaved, and sometimes a fund raiser-administrator for his synagogue. The various Rabbinic organizations can guide and advise their members on religious matters, but by and large each Rabbi has the right to make the final decision for himself and his congregation. In Israel, Britain, and a few other countries there is a Chief Rabbi, but no such position exists in the U.S. Rabbis have served as chaplains with the armed forces of the U.S. since the Civil War. Sephardic and eastern Jews generally call their Rabbi a Haham ("sage").

RAIN. The success of crops in Israel is heavily dependent on rain and dew in season, and for this reason there are special prayers recited for *geshem* ("rain") and *tal* ("dew").

RAINBOW. After the flood of Biblical antiquity, God placed a rainbow in the sky as part of his covenant with Noah. Orthodox Jews, upon seeing a rainbow, are enjoined to recite a special blessing in which God is thanked for remembering the covenant and "keeps his promise" not to flood the world again.

RAM'S HORN. *See* Shofar.

RASHI. (Full name Rabbi Shlomo Yitzhaki.) Rashi lived in France in the 11th and 12th centuries; although he earned his livelihood as a vintner, he devoted a lifetime to producing what is considered the

ר׳ שלמה יצחקי רש״י

נולד ד׳ תת נם׳ ד׳ תתסה

Rashi

greatest commentary on the Bible and the Talmud—a commentary studied by virtually every beginning, intermediate, and advanced student of the Bible and the Talmud. His commentary on the Bible, the first printed Hebrew book, was issued in 1475.

RASHI SCRIPT. Cursive version of the Hebrew alphabet employed by Spanish Jews and used today in Rabbinic commentaries.

READING OF THE LAW. (*Kri'at ha-Torah* in Hebrew.) A section of the Torah is read in synagogue at the morning and afternoon service of Sabbath, festivals, and on Mondays and Thursdays. The Torah cycle reading begins and ends on the festival of Simhat Torah, when the scrolls of the Law are carried around the synagogue for all congregants to kiss, and amid much rejoicing that the cycle has been completed and starts anew. A minyan is required if the Torah is to be read from. The reader is known as the *baal kriyah* ("master of reading"), and is required to be able to read without help from vowels or punctuation, which are not included in the scrolls of the Law. He is also expected to be able to read aloud in a traditional chant, following prescribed cantillation notes. A man called to the reading of the Torah takes the corner of his tallit, touches the place where the reader has stopped, recites a blessing, and does the same when his section of reading is completed. In recent years Jewish feminists have been pressing for permission to be called to the reading of the Law; this is now optional with individual Conservative congregations. The highlight of the bar mitzvah ceremony is the young man's being called to the Torah, reciting the appropriate blessings and usually chanting the accompanying Prophetic portion.

REBBE. Term combining respect and endearment used for Hasidic leaders (who may or may not be ordained Rabbis).

RECONSTRUCTIONISM. American-born religious movement led by Rabbi Mordecai M. Kaplan, which aims at eliminating the supernatural and the concept of chosen people from Judaism, concentrating on the ethical precepts, and striving for Israel's becoming a worldwide spiritual homeland for all Jews. Judaism is seen as an evolving civilization responding to the changes all around it.

RECONSTRUCTIONIST RABBINICAL SEMINARY. Rabbinic seminary of the Reconstructionist movement, in Philadelphia.

RED HEIFER. A Biblical injunction called for the sacrifice of a blemish-free red heifer whose ashes (mixed with water) were sprinkled over those contaminated through contact with the dead. Rabbis ex-

A page from a festival prayer book
depicting the red heifer. Italy, 1441.

plained that this ancient statute was one of those
listed in the Bible for which no logical explanation
could be offered.

REFORM JUDAISM. Major wing of the Jewish religion. Its advocates call for modifying Orthodox customs and practices they consider out of step with contemporary life. Halachah, Jewish religious law, is
viewed by the Reform movement as changeable, re-
vocable, and adaptable—while Orthodox (and to a

large extent, Conservative) Jews view Halachah as fundamental and not to be tampered with. Reform began in Germany in the early 19th century, and was launched in its present form in the U.S. in the 1870s. There are more than 600 Reform temples in the U.S. with a membership in excess of 1 million families.

RELIGIOUS PARTIES. A number of political parties in Israel are organized along religious lines, and form voting blocs. Chief among these are the Mizrachi and Agudat Israel, the former now known as the National Religious party and the latter having a labor-oriented offshoot, Poalei Agudat Israel.

REMNANT OF ISRAEL. (*She'arit Israel* in Hebrew.) Throughout the Bible the people of Israel are warned about returning to an ethical way of life, with catastrophic punishments to follow if they do not. Nevertheless, there remains in all these dire prophecies a hope and promise that all Jews will not be punished, but that a remnant will remain from whom the Jewish people will grow again.

RENDING OF CLOTHES. (*Kriyah* in Hebrew.) Tearing one's clothes as a mourning sign is mentioned in the Bible. Until recently, mourners who had lost a close relative had a cut made in their garments, indicating their bereavement. This is still done by Orthodox Jews, but has largely been replaced by other mourning signs such as wearing a black armband or ribbon in the lapel. Orthodox Jews also rend their garments upon hearing of a communal or national Jewish disaster, or when a scroll of the Law has been destroyed by fire.

REPENTANCE. (*Teshuvah* in Hebrew.) Judaism is a firm believer in repentance. It is one of the basic 613 commandments, and one of the three factors stressed in High Holy Day prayers (the other two being prayer and charity). In the Jewish view a man may be possessed of an evil inclination and commit a wrong, but this can be forgiven if he repents and does good deeds thereafter and appeases the injured party.

RESPONSA. Literature that has grown up around the questions and answers of Jewish religious law as interpreted through the generations. Rabbis are still engaged in answering questions that relate to Jewish law and that flow from the new technological and scientific developments of the day. A typical question for an Orthodox Jew might be whether he is violating the Sabbath law by standing outside a store window featuring a television show and watching the program without having paid admission or flicked on the electric switch (both of which are prohibited).

RESURRECTION. (*Tehiyat ha-metim* in Hebrew.) The question of resurrection has exercised Jewish religious thinkers for many centuries. Belief in resurrection is one of the 13 principles of faith enunciated by Maimonides, although most modern Rabbis interpret this to mean resurrection of the soul. There are Jews who believe in the literal resurrection of the dead in a Messianic age, but most Jews have a more skeptical (but perhaps also hopeful) attitude.

RETRIBUTION. Conviction that God rewards the righteous and punishes the wicked is a basic Jewish tenet. Simple happiness, Jewish tradition holds, is reward enough for a life of good deeds, while sorrow is the fate of the evildoer. Rabbinic commentators stressed that reward and punishment may have to wait for *olam haba* ("the next world").

RIGHTEOUSNESS. Combination of uprightness and honesty, and freedom from sinfulness, deceit, and evil. One who is righteous is called a tzaddik (*tsedek* means, broadly, "righteousness," but also means "justice"). The Bible stresses the pursuit of righteous ways; when God and Abraham concluded a convenant, Abraham's descendants were adjured to "keep the way of the Lord, to do righteousness and justice."

RIMMONIM. (Hebrew for "pomegranates.") Silver or gold minicrowns, usually round in shape, and often with small tinkling bells dangling, placed atop the rollers of the scrolls of the Law when the scrolls are carried through the synagogue.

RISHONIM AND ACHARONIM. (Hebrew for "the first ones, the last ones.") The Rishonim include the forefathers of the Jewish people and the Major and

Silver rimmonim.
Italy, c. 1600.

Silver rimmonim.
Germany, c. 1725.

Silver-plated rimmonim.
Middle Eastern, 19th century.

Minor Prophets. The term was also used to describe the codifiers of Rabbinic law up to the 16th century. The codifiers who have followed, after the appearance of the *Shulchan Aruch*, are called Acharonim.

ROSH HASHANAH. (Hebrew for "beginning of the year.") The Jewish New Year takes place on the 1st and 2d days of Tishri, ushering in a period of ten days of awe, culminating in Yom Kippur. Rosh Hashanah is also called the Day of Judgment and the Day of Remembrance. Tradition says that the world was born on Rosh Hashanah. The holiday is synagogue-oriented, with most congregations adding large public rooms to accommodate the overflow attendance. The shofar is sounded on Rosh Hashanah, unless New Year falls on the Sabbath. Home observances include the use of a round hallah (Sabbath bread), denoting the eternity of life, dipped in honey in the hope that the new year will be sweet. Some Jews still practice tashlich—they walk to a nearby body of flowing water and empty their pockets of lint into it, symbolizing the casting off of their sins. More than other Jewish holidays, Rosh Hashanah has a universalistic orientation, with the congregants praying for peace and tranquility for all mankind.

ROSH YESHIVAH. Head of an academy devoted to Biblical and Talmudic studies.

SABBATH. Weekly rest day observed from Friday sunset through Saturday sunset. One of the Ten Commandments is to "remember the Sabbath day, to keep it holy." A day a week is set aside for rest, first, as a reminder that God created the world in six days and rested on the seventh; therefore, the Sabbath is a weekly reminder of the fact that although man administers the world, it is God's creation and must be cared for in his spirit. Second, the social implications are easily discernible: a seventh part of the week is set aside for spiritual, physical rest in an atmosphere of maximum tranquility, with every person in the household (including servants) required to rest. Thus the Sabbath is seen as a 24-hour period of prayer, study, festive meals, song, and renewal, and surcease from daily labor. As has been said about the Jewish observance of the Sabbath, "More than Israel has kept the Sabbath, the Sabbath has kept Israel." At services there is a special Sabbath ritual, and congregants are expected to attend in their best attire. At home, meals are especially prepared, with wine on Friday eve, and a Sabbath bread called hallah for the entire day. Candles are kindled before the Sabbath, and the candlesticks remain in place through the day. In more Orthodox homes, zemirot—festive songs with gentle melodies—accompany the meals. On the Sabbath, fathers are likely to discuss the week's studies with their children. Second only to Yom Kippur in importance, the Sabbath, when properly understood and observed, becomes a day of spiritual refreshment and pleasure.

SABBATICAL YEAR. (*Shemittah* in Hebrew.) According to the Bible, every seventh year "the land must keep Sabbath unto the Lord." Land must lie fallow in the Shemittah year; if anything should grow on it, it may be taken by passersby. The point of this law, Rabbinic authorities say, was to indicate to the Jewish people that the ownership of the Holy Land was conditional—they had to continue to obey God's Law. Some Orthodox Jews in Israel observe the law by transferring ownership to a non-Jew during the Sabbatical year; others permit the land to remain fallow and produce income from other sources. Modern ecologists maintain that the concept of the land being given a rest every seventh year is sound agronomy.

SADDUCEES. Small sect that flourished during the time of the Second Temple. Some historians claim they were mostly politically rather than religiously motivated. The sect members were closely associated with the priestly families, unlike the Pharisees, who sought to disseminate the teachings of the oral law to the masses of Israelites.

SAFED. Small mountain town in Galilee that became a center for Jewish mystics. It is considered one of the four holy cities in Israel, the others being Jerusalem, Hebron, and Tiberias.

SALTING. Since the Bible forbids the consumption of blood, all meats placed on the table must be rid of any blood vestiges. This is accomplished by soaking the meat in water for a half hour, sprinkling salt on it and letting it stand for another hour, then rinsing. Meat broiled directly over a flame does not require soaking and salting. (Liver cannot be salted—it can only be made kosher by broiling.)

SAMARITANS. Small sect of people who claim descent from the ten lost tribes. Their Jewish practices are comparable to those of the Karaites (q.v.). Rabbinic authorities do not regard Samaritans as Jews and Jews are not allowed to intermarry with them. Samaritans reside primarily in Nablus and in Holon, Israel.

SAMBATYON. Legendary river, made of stones and rubble rather than water, that flows six days of the week and rests on the Sabbath. Legend adds that on the farther side of the river voyagers will find the ten lost tribes.

SANDAK. Person who is given the honor of holding a child on his knees during the circumcision ceremony. Usually he is the child's grandfather.

SANHEDRIN. Supreme religious and judicial body of the Jews during the Temple period. Criminal and capital offenses came before the Sanhedrin (Great Assembly), but its chief task was to adjudicate matters of religious competence. The Sanhedrin remained in existence until the 7th century c.e. A group of Jewish notables convened by Napoleon in 1807 to confirm the Jews' loyalty to the Napoleonic code was called the Sanhedrin. From time to time religious leaders have voiced the hope that a new Sanhedrin would be reconstituted so that religious questions could be reviewed and decided on.

SCRIBE. A sofer is a religiously oriented scribe who copies the Torah, and also copies the short prayers inserted into a pair of tefillin and a mezuzah.

SCROLL OF THE LAW. (*Sefer Torah* in Hebrew.) The Torah written by a scribe on parchment or vellum, and used for public reading in the synagogue. The parchment is from the leather of a ritually clean animal, and each section is sewed together to form one long scroll with threads made from tendons of clean animals. There are no vowels or punctuation, but sec-

Torah scroll. Mediterranean, late 18th century.

tions are indicated by spacing. The scroll of the Law is housed in the holy ark. A scroll that is worn out may not be destroyed but is either buried in a special ceremony or is stored in the synagogue's genizah, or storeroom. If a synagogue is burning, the scrolls must be saved first after people. If a scroll is dropped accidentally, all those present are obliged to fast.

SCROLLS, THE FIVE. Five books in the Holy Writings section of the Bible are classed as the five scrolls and are read from during specific times of the year: the Book of Esther is read on Purim; Lamentations, on Tisha B'Av; Ecclesiastes, on the Sabbath of Sukkoth week; the Song of Songs, on the Sabbath of Passover week; and Ruth, on Shavuoth.

SEDER. *See* Passover.

SELICHOT. Penitential prayers recited around midnight on the Saturday night preceding the High Holy Days.

SEMICHA. Term used for ordination of a Rabbi. It is derived from the Biblical account of Moses transferring authority to Joshua by placing his hands on Joshua's head.

SEMITES. Group of related peoples whose domains stretched from the Mediterranean coast to modern Iran and Armenia, and included Arabs, Hebrews, Phoenicians, Babylonians, and Assyrians. According to the Bible all these Semitic peoples descended from Noah's son Shem.

SEPHARDIM. Jews of Spain, Portugal, and other countries located in the Mediterranean basin area are known as Sephardim, or Sephardic Jews. They differ from central and east European Jews in language (Yiddish was unknown to them, but they spoke Ladino, a mixture of Spanish, Latin, and some Hebrew, and, like Yiddish, written in Hebrew characters) and in minor religious rites. Some of the greatest Jewish figures in history were Sephardic—Maimonides, Judah Halevi, Ibn Gabirol.

SEPTUAGINT. Oldest existing translation of the Bible, believed to have been done in the 3d century B.C.E. by some 70 scholars who translated the Hebrew into Greek in Alexandria. The translation was a great artistic and scholarly achievement but a few scholars believe it hastened the disappearance of Hebrew-speaking Jews in the then flourishing Jewish community of Alexandria.

SEUDAH SHLISHIT. Small repast eaten by Jews in the synagogue in the fading hours of the Sabbath afternoon, usually accompanied by a bit of Torah study and singing. Also known as shalosh seudah.

SEUDATH MITZVAH. Commandment meal, or a festive meal accompanying a religious occasion such as a wedding, bar mitzvah, or circumcision, when it is considered a religious duty to join in the festivities.

17TH OF TAMMUZ. Fast day marking Titus's breaching of the walls of Jerusalem in the year 70; Moses' smashing of the first tablets of the law; the end of daily sacrifices in the Temple; an idol being erected in the Temple in the reign of Manassah; and the scrolls of the Law being burned by Apostomus. A three-week mourning period from the 17th of Tammuz to Tisha B'Av is observed.

SEX. Judaism takes a frank and open attitude toward sex, and recognizes the strength of the sexual drive. It believes sex is not intrinsically sinful or shameful but should be confined to marriage and governed by certain set rules. Sodomy, pederasty, adultery, and incest are branded as capital offenses condemned as heinous crimes against God. Wearing the clothes of the opposite sex is forbidden, lest it lead to promiscuity. Women may wear slacks, however, if they are cut for women. Celibacy was discouraged by the Rabbis.

SHABBAT HAGADOL. (Hebrew for, literally, "the Great Sabbath.") The Sabbath before Passover. On this day and on the Sabbath between Rosh Hashanah and Yom Kippur the Rabbi usually delivers a special sermon.

SHABBES GOY. Yiddish expression for a non-Jew who was hired to carry out certain tasks on the Sabbath that a Jew could not do, lighting a fire in cold weather, relieving an animal in pain, etc. Arrangements with the non-Jew should be made prior to the Sabbath.

SHACHARIT. Morning service, from the word *shachar* ("dawn").

SHADAI. One of the names of God. The word is used in the mezuzah affixed to a doorpost.

SHADCHAN. Marriage broker. Such a vocation was essential in the Middle Ages when travel was highly restricted. The marriage broker still functions in Israel, and to a slight extent in the U.S.

SHALOM ALEICHEM. Traditional greeting between

Jews. It means "Peace be unto you," and usually is responded to with, *"Aleichem Shalom"* ("Unto you may there be peace").

SHALOM BAYIT. (Hebrew for, literally, "peace of house.") Connotes tranquillity and domestic felicity in a Jewish household. A Talmudic maxim says: "Where there is peace between husband and wife, the divine presence dwells among them."

SHAMMASH. Sexton of a synagogue, whose learning often is extensive if not as complete as that of the Rabbi. The same word is used for the ninth candle used during Hanukkah to light the eight candles of the festival.

SHAS. Abbreviation for the six orders of the Mishnah; commonly used today to mean the entire Talmud.

SHATNEZ. According to the Bible, garments containing mixed wool and linen may not be worn. Such a garment is said to contain shatnez. In some Orthodox communities clothing stores sell garments that are guaranteed to be free of shatnez.

SHAVUOTH. Feast of weeks, one of the pilgrim festivals listed in the Bible, celebrated two days (6th and 7th of Sivan) outside Israel but only one day in Israel. It falls exactly seven weeks after Passover, hence its name. The festival is celebrated as the time of the giving of the law on Mount Sinai, and simultaneously as a holiday of the first fruits, which in Temple days were brought to the Temple. The synagogue service includes a solemn reading of the Ten Commandments, and reading the Book of Ruth, emphasizing the acceptance of God's law by a proselyte. Many agricultural settlements in Israel have instituted colorful ceremonies marking the first harvest.

SHECHINA. Divine presence.

SHECHITAH. Ritual slaughter. Basically it consists of cutting the windpipe and gullet with a razor-thin instrument so as to minimize the animal's suffering. (Fish, of course, and locusts permissible as food do not require shechitah.) The ritual slaughterer, known as a shochet, is required to be an observant Jew thoroughly experienced in his craft. After each use the cutting tool must be examined carefully to ascertain that it has no imperfections or notches. At certain times and in some communities ritual slaughter has been condemned by anti-Semites or by humane societies spokesmen, but scientific evidence has been developed to show that the method is humane.

SHEITL. *See* Wig.

SHEMA. Word that begins the verse *"Shema Yisrael"* ("Hear, O Israel, the Lord our God, the Lord is One"). Taken from the Bible, the phrase is incorporated into the morning and evening services. The verse expresses Judaism's central belief in the unity of God. Martyrs through the ages met their death with the words of the shema on their lips.

SHEMINI ATZERET. Eighth day of solemn assembly, part of the festival of Sukkoth. A prayer for rain is offered on this day. In Israel the holiday is combined with Simhat Torah.

SHEVA BERACHOT. (Hebrew for "seven blessings.") Special series of benedictions recited immediately after the wedding ceremony by the assembled guests. The blessings are usually recited for seven days after the wedding during grace after meals whenever a minyan is present.

SHEVAT. Fifth month of the Jewish calendar in which Jewish Arbor Day falls.

SHIELD OF DAVID. *See* Magen David.

SHIRAYIM. (Hebrew for "remainders.") Food left over after a meal by a Hasidic Rabbi. His followers

Engraved shofar. Europe, 18th century.

scramble to obtain a scrap. They believe that this will endow them with some of their Rabbi's holy powers.

SHIVAH. Week-long mourning period following the funeral of a loved one. The mourner sits on a low bench, unshod, unshaven, recites the mourner's kaddish prayer, and is comforted by friends and relatives who are obliged to visit him during his bereavement.

SHOCHET. Ritual slaughterer. *See* Shechitah.

SHOFAR. Ram's horn sounded during the High Holy Days and at the end of the morning service in the month of Elul. During Bible days the shofar was used for ceremonial occasions such as anointing a king or proclaiming a Jubilee year. At times it was sounded as a warning of attack. Various explanations are given for the blasting of the shofar, among which is that of Maimonides, who said its message was: "Awake you sleepers from your sleep, and you that are in slumber, rouse yourselves. Consider your ways, remember God, turn to him." In Orthodox communities the shofar is blown on Friday afternoon to announce the ushering

The sound of the ram's horn
signals the approach of the Jewish New Year.

in of the Sabbath. In Israel the swearing in of the president is accompanied by shofar blasts. The man (or sometimes youth) who sounds the shofar for the High Holy Days is called a *Baal tekiah,* and must play certain carefully prescribed notes.

SHROUD. (*Tahrichin* in Hebrew.) The Jewish burial garment is a simple white shroud. A deceased male is covered with his own tallit, or prayer shawl, and is buried in it.

SHTETL (or Stetl). One of the small rural villages inhabited almost exclusively by Jews, most of whom barely eked out a livelihood, that existed in eastern Europe, primarily Russia, Poland, and the Baltic states, for several centuries. Cut off from the mainstream of society, the Jews lived devoutly religious lives with study of the Bible and the Talmud a major source of their spiritual and intellectual sustenance.

SHULCHAN ARUCH. Most widely current code of Jewish law. Prepared by Joseph Karo and in use since the 16th century.

SHTREIML. A fur-trimmed hat often worn by ultra-Orthodox as well as some Hasidic Jews, dating back several centuries ago in Poland.

SICK, VISITS TO THE. The concept of *bikur holim*—visiting the sick—is strongly entrenched in Judaism. The Talmud taught that whoever "visits the sick reduces his ailment by one-sixtieth." Societies whose chief purpose is to visit and comfort the ailing have been a feature of organized Jewish life for many generations.

SIDDUR. (Hebrew for, literally, "orderly arrangement.") (The special prayer book for the High Holy Days is a mahzor.) The word dates from the 9th century; there are variations on the first siddur, attributed to Amram Gaon. Many of the liturgical selections in use date back to Temple days, and some of the prayers in use today are believed to be substantially the same as those used in ancient times. Prayer books used by Orthodox, Conservative, Reform, Ashkenazic, and Sephardic Jews are by no means uniform, but major portions are identical.

SIDRAH. Weekly portion of the Torah read aloud during Sabbath (and festival) services, so divided that the reading begins and ends on Simhat Torah, then begins anew. Each sidrah is usually named for the initial word. Some congregations call the sidrah a parashah.

SIMHAT BAT. A relatively new ceremony that has developed in recent years in which the birth of an infant girl is celebrated at a festive meal, during which the child's Hebrew name is announced, with the rabbi offering a special prayer for her well-being and for the health of the mother. The Hebrew term means "Joy of a Daughter."

SIMHAT TORAH. Festival of the rejoicing of the law Concluding day of the festival of Sukkoth. The yearly cycle of readings from the Torah is concluded and begun again on this day, which features dancing with the scrolls of the Law in the synagogue, children waving flags, and general merriment at the happy occasion. The scrolls are carried around the synagogue

Woodcut of a Simhat Torah flag. Poland, 19th century.

seven times, and every adult in the congregation is expected to make the circuit. Many women today are also carrying the Torah during the festivities. In some synagogues the festival is occasion for unusual behavior, e.g., deliberately not following the cantor's leading of the singing—but it's all done in a once-a-year fun spirit.

SIN. In the Jewish view a sin consists of any departure from God's way, or any transgression of the divine commandments. Three major categories of sinful behavior are listed: a *het,* an unknowing sin; an *avon,* a sin committed with advance knowledge; and a *pesha,* a rebellious transgression. No sin, according to Jewish tradition, is unforgivable, but to be pardoned the sinner must repent, confess to God, make restitution (where this is applicable), and give charity.

SINAI, MOUNT. Also known as Horeb, a mountain located in the Sinai Peninsula at the foot of which the Israelites who fled from Egyptian slavery encamped, and where Moses ascended to the top to receive the Ten Commandments. The precise location of the mountain is not known.

SIVAN. Ninth month of the Jewish year during which Shavuoth falls.

SIYUM. Celebration marking the completion of study of a full tractate of the Talmud. Another kind of siyum is a celebration marking conclusion of the writing by a scribe of a scroll of the Law. Every man present has the privilege of inscribing one letter of the scroll.

SLANDER. *See Leshon ha-Ra.*

SLAVERY. Although the Bible and Talmud accepted the system of slavery as a normal part of the then existing economic and social system, every effort was made to institute humane treatment of the enslaved. A Jew was forbidden to sell himself for life but could do so for a brief time if his economic situation warranted it. After six years Jewish slaves had to be freed, as they had to be in the Jubilee year, whichever came first. Any ill treatment of a slave (such as brought about the loss of an eye or a tooth), both Jewish and non-Jewish, resulted in automatic release from bondage. The Talmud taught that whoever "acquires a slave to himself acquires a master to himself."

SOCIAL JUSTICE. The plea for social justice is a common theme among all the Prophets, and is also seen in Biblical legislation. Society and individuals were commanded to care for the poor, widows, and orphans, and to avoid talebearing, malice, and vengeance. Those who were outwardly pietistic but did not practice social justice were condemned in the harshest terms. A nation's continued survival, the Bible teaches, depends on national righteousness and social justice.

SONG OF SONGS. The first of the five scrolls, the book is outwardly a superb collection of love poetry, the erotic exchange of two lovers. Rabbi Akiva, pressing for its inclusion in the Bible in the face of opposition by those who held it to be too secular, said it was an allegorical description of the love affair between the Jewish people and God. King Solomon is believed to have written the book.

SPICES. Spices were used extensively in ancient times as condiments and as perfumes. It was customary to burn spices after a meal and recite a blessing before smelling them—this is the probable origin for sniffing spices at the havdalah (q.v.) service.

STAR OF DAVID. See Magen David.

STERILIZATION. Castration is forbidden by the Bible, as is marriage to a man who has been "crushed or maimed in his privy parts." Also forbidden, except in certain circumstances, is drinking from the "cup of sterility," an oral contraceptive known in ancient days and referred to frequently in the Talmud. Sterilization of women was also banned. The only time such an operation may be performed is to save the life of the individual involved.

STRANGER. In ancient times strangers in a community had little legal protection. The Bible cautioned the Israelites to show every consideration to the "stranger within thy gates" and treat him like an Israelite. To qualify for the protection offered by the

Jewish community the stranger had to abide by the Noachian Laws.

STUDY. Studying the Torah daily is regarded as a positive commandment. Rabbinic authorities said that a man should give all his free time to study, with one-third to the Torah, one-third to the Talmud, and one-third to the Mishnah. Education was considered so important that in many communities the wife went out to work while her husband pursued his studies.

SUICIDE. Because Judaism believes that an individual is not the unlimited master of his own life, suicide is regarded as murder and is strictly forbidden. Until recently a suicide had to be buried in a separate part of the cemetery, but a recent ruling has said that suicides are not of sound mind and can be interred normally.

SUKKAH. Booth in which the Jews were commanded to live for seven days so as to remember the Israelites who resided in booths during their exodus from Egypt. The sukkah may be of any material; it must be at least 10 but not more than 20 cubits high; and its roof must be covered with boughs, through which the stars are visible. Jews today who observe the sukkah law generally eat their meals there; most synagogues construct a sukkah on the premises, and after services on Sukkoth the congregants are invited to enter for light refreshments. Traditionally the sukkah is decorated with a variety of fruits and vegetables, since Sukkoth is also the harvest festival.

SUKKOTH. Festival celebrating the completion of the harvest. It reminds Jews of the wanderings of their ancestors in the wilderness before entering the promised land. A seven-day festival, it is followed immediately by Shmini Atzeret and Simhat Torah, making this a long, joyous celebration.

SUPERSTITION. The Bible specifically prohibits magic, divination, and other superstitious practices. Nevertheless, some practices continued through the generations and have persisted to our own day. A visitor to a loved one's grave who leaves a small stone on the tombstone is practicing a superstitious rite, as

ולקחתם לכם ביום הראשון פרי עץ הדר כפות תמרים וענף עץ עבות וערבי
נחל ושמחתם לפני ד' אלהיכם שבעת ימים: ויקרא כג מ

Etching depicting the procession in
synagogue with etrog and lulav.

is a mother who exclaims, when her child is praised, "May the evil eye not touch him" ("*Kein ain-ha-ra*").

SWAYING. Worshipers can often be seen swaying during the standing part of the service, or while reading aloud from the Torah. Judah ha-Levi, a great medieval poet and philosopher, explained this by saying that because of a shortage of books, scholars had to keep moving around to look over their colleagues' shoulders. Vigorous swaying during prayer may be seen especially in a Hasidic synagogue and is called in Yiddish, shuckling.

SYNAGOGUE. Although the origin of the word for a Jewish house of worship is not known, it is clear that a synagogue has three major functions: as a house of prayer (Bet Tefilah), house of study (Bet Midrash), and house of assembly (Bet Knesset). At the time of the Second Temple a formal synagogue was already a well-established Jewish institution. Unlike the Holy Temple, a synagogue is directed by its own members, not by a hierarchy of priests. The Rabbi, who is chosen for his learning, piety, and spiritual leadership qualities, can be dismissed by the members; the cantor is regarded as a *shaliach tzibur* ("emissary of the people"), whose voice expresses the sentiments, hopes, and prayers of all the congregants. The main furnishing of a synagogue is the holy ark, where the scrolls of the Law are kept. Traditionally, the main wall faces east, toward Jerusalem. Synagogues have been erected in practically every corner of the world; there is no architectural guideline followed when a new one is planned. In the U.S. the synagogue has evolved into a social, communal, and educational center, as well as a house of prayer.

TABERNACLE. (*Ohel Moed* in Hebrew.) Portable sanctuary used by the Israelites from the time of Moses until construction of the first Holy Temple by King Solomon. The central, most revered section contained the ark of the covenant, containing the tablets of the law, on which were inscribed the Ten Commandments.

TABERNACLES, FESTIVAL OF. Third of the pilgrim festivals referred to in the Bible. *See* Sukkoth.

TABLETS OF THE LAW. (*Luhot ha-Brit* in Hebrew.) Two stone tablets on which, according to Bible tradition, the Ten Commandments were inscribed on Mount Sinai at the time of Moses' ascent, as proof of God's covenant with Israel. Exodus describes the tablets as being written by "the finger of God." The tablets were deposited in the holy of holies section of the Temple built by Solomon. Most of the holy arks in modern synagogues are decorated with a representation of the tablets.

TAGIN. Crownlike flourishes added to the Hebrew letters used in the handwritten copy of the scroll of the Law. Similar embellishments also appear in handwritten scrolls of the mezuzah and tefillin. Kabbalists attributed mystical significance to these decorative additions.

TAHANUN. A special prayer for forgiveness recited after the amidah service, on weekday mornings and afternoons, except when a joyful event is celebrated in the synagogue.

TAHARAT MISHPACHAH. (Hebrew for "family purity.") A whole series of laws listing permissible and illicit marital relationships and setting down guidelines for a life of family purity is included in the Halachah. Many of these laws deal with what times husbands and wives can have sexual relationships, based on the wife's menstrual period. *See also* Family; Mikveh; Nidah.

TAHRICHIN. *See* Shroud.

TAKKANAH. (pl. takkanoth). Ordinance promulgated by local Rabbinic authorities in post-Talmudic times, meant to bolster religious and moral life, and supplementing a Torah regulation. The first takkanah, which preceded Talmudic days, is said to have been that of Moses, who ordered the reading of the Law at weekly Sabbath (and festival) services, as well

Embroidered silk prayer shawl. Russia, 19th century.

as on the first day of the new month. Typical of the takkanoth were those of 11th-century Rabbi Gershom ben Judah, who ruled that letters to others could not be opened, and ordered an end to polygamy.

TALLIT. Prayer shawl, a large four-cornered shawl-like garment with fringes at the corners, worn by men during morning services. Traditionally made of wool, the tallit may also be made of silk or a synthetic material; recently a tallit in the U.S. was manufactured from denim. In some congregations the tallit is worn only by married men, while in others young boys, especially those at children's services, wear small versions of the adult tallit. It is customary for a father to present his son with a tallit as part of the bar mitzvah ceremony. A very recent phenomenon is the demand by some feminists to wear a tallit, to which a small number of synagogues have acceded. The tallit is worn at evening services once a year—at the Yom Kippur (Kol Nidre) eve service, and throughout the day on Yom Kippur.

TALMID CHACHAM. (Hebrew for "disciple of a sage.") Refers to a scholar, young or old, whose study of Torah and the Talmud is never-ending. Modern usage includes any person who is truly learned because he never ceases learning. A Talmudic maxim states that a bastard "who is a talmid chacham takes precedence over a High Priest who is an ignoramus."

TALMUD. Comprehensive designation for the Mishnah and the Gemara as a single unit. There are Babylonian and Jerusalem Talmuds, the latter a commentary on 39 of the 63 tractates of the Mishnah developed in academies in ancient Israel, whose editing was completed in the 4th century. The Babylonian Talmud, generally considered more precise, was set down in Babylonian centers of learning between the 3d and 5th centuries and covers 37 tractates of the Mishnah. Two-thirds of the Babylonian Talmud is Aggadah, compared to the Jerusalem Talmud's one-sixth. The Babylonian Talmud was written in Hebrew and Aramaic, while the Jerusalem Talmud is in Aramaic with Greek and other foreign terms included. The Talmud is a storehouse of Jewish history and customs, as well as laws; the Babylonian version, three times as long as the Jerusalem, is generally considered superior. The Babylonian Talmud has been translated into several languages, including English, and has itself been the subject of numerous commentaries. The scholars who prepared the Gemara are known as the Amoraim. The Mishnah consists of six orders, each divided into tractates, and each of these subdivided. A legal codification of basic Jewish law, dating to 200, the Mishnah contains the basic oral law transmitted throughout the generations from the time of the giving of the Torah. Its divisions are (1) Zeraim ("Seeds"), dealing with agricultural laws; (2) Moed ("Appointed Times"), laws of festivals and feasts; (3) Nashim ("Women"), marriage, divorce, vows; (4) Nezikin ("Damages"), civil and criminal law; (5) Kodoshim ("Holy Things"), primarily Temple rituals; and (6) Taharot ("Purity"), laws of ritual purity and impurity. The Mishnah was recorded in Hebrew, although it differs from modern Hebrew and includes Greek, Latin, and some Aramaic. Broadly, the Talmud contains laws, legends, ethics, comments on philosophy, medicine, agriculture, astronomy, and hygiene—making it a perpetual source of study for generations of Jews.

TALMUD, BURNING OF. In the 13th century, goaded by an apostate who claimed the Talmud contained blasphemies against Jesus (totally untrue, of course), 24 carloads of the Talmud were burned in France. In later centuries, burning of the Talmud incidents took place in Italy, Poland, and other countries.

TALMUD TORAH. (Hebrew for "study of the Torah.") A somewhat dated term used to describe the school where youngsters receive a religious education, with either the community as a whole or a particular congregation responsible for funding.

TAMMUZ. Tenth month of the Jewish calendar.

TANNA (pl. Tannaim; Aramaic for "one who studies and teaches.") Term used frequently in the Mishnah.

TANYA. Classic work of the Hasidic movement, written by Shneor Zalman, who founded the Habad movement. "Habad" is an acronym for three Hebrew words setting forth the movement's philosophy: *hochma* ("faith"), *binah* ("contemplation and study"), and *daat* ("true knowledge" of God).

TARGUM. Aramaic translation of the Bible. It was ordered by Ezra the Scribe because the everyday language of the Jews was Aramaic. The best-known translation into Aramaic was that of Onkelos, said to have been a proselyte, which is still found in many Bibles.

TARYAG. Term used for the 613 commandments Jews are required to obey. The word is the letter equivalent of the number 613.

TASHLICH. (Hebrew for "cast off.") Custom whereby Orthodox Jews, on the first day of Rosh Hashanah, proceed to a nearby body of water and "cast off" their sins by emptying their pockets and symbolically throwing the lint into the water.

TASHMISHEI KEDUSHAH. (Hebrew for "appurtenances of holiness.") Religious articles and synagogue appurtenances, e.g., the shofar, tallit, and ornaments of the Torah, which are to be treated with reverence.

TEFILLIN. (Hebrew for "phylacteries.") Based on a Biblical command, boys over 13 and men are required to don a pair of tefillin each morning at services (except on Sabbath and festivals). The tefillin consist of a small leather case, one for the head and another for the arm, and contain Biblical injunctions for their use. They are held in place by leather thongs, with the one for the arm resting on the inner side of the forearm, and the thong entwined down the arm and knotted loosely on the fingers. The purpose of the tefillin is to direct the user's thoughts to God. Maimonides wrote that "so long as the tefillin are on the head and arm of a man, he is humble and God-fearing, he turns his heart exclusively to words of truth and justice." The knot on the hand is formed in the shape of the letter shin, representing the name of God, Shadai.

TEHINNOT. Simple devotional prayers, generally in Yiddish, meant for recitation by women—who in an-

Silver tefillin case. Poland, 19th century.

cient times did not receive the same education as men. The term also referred to personal prayers and supplications added to the standard service, usually dealing with health, livelihood, and the like.

TEN COMMANDMENTS. Commandments given by God to Moses on Mount Sinai, considered by the Rabbis to be the quintessence of Jewish law and life. There are two versions in the Bible, one in the Book of Exodus and another in Deuteronomy, with minor differences such as the reason for the observance of Sabbath. Some commentators claim the first version represents the first set, smashed by Moses when he descended from the mountaintop and found the Israelites worshiping the golden calf, and the second version is the second set he brought down after a second trip to the mountain's peak. The reading of the Decalogue is a high point of the Shavuoth service, when the congregation rises as the commandments are read aloud from the Torah.

TEN TRIBES. Traditional name for the inhabitants of the northern kingdom of Israel. Refers to the tribes of Reuben, Simeon, Dan, Naftali, Gad, Asher, Issachar, Zebulun, Ephraim and Menashe, which were deported in the 8th century to Assyria and other parts of the Assyrian Empire, where they were assimilated and lost their identity. In Jewish legends the "ten lost tribes" continued to live on in a mythical country. (See also *Twelve Tribes*.)

TENAIM. (Hebrew for "condition.") Document of betrothal between the father of the bride and the bridegroom, laying down the terms for the forthcoming marriage, including a clause specifying a penalty for default by either party.

TEREFAH. (Hebrew for "not kosher.") The word stems from the Biblical injunction against eating the meat of an animal that has been torn or mauled, but today refers to any food that is not conformable to Jewish dietary laws.

TETRAGRAMMATON. Name of God consisting of the four Hebrew letters yod, heh, vav, and heh, which is never pronounced as spelled ("Adonai" is substituted). During the Temple period the High Priest enunciated the name in full, but only on the Day of Atonement.

TEVET. Fourth month of the Jewish year.

TEVILAH. *See* Immersion.

THANKSGIVING, BLESSING OF. (*Birkat ha-Gomel* in Hebrew.) Special benediction offering thanks for delivery from imprisonment, for recovery from sickness, and after crossing a sea or desert. The blessing is usually offered in synagogue when a person is called to the reading of the Law.

13 ATTRIBUTES. Based on a Biblical source, Rabbinic authorities said that God has 13 attributes of mercy.

13 PRINCIPLES OF FAITH. Dogmas of Judaism, as enunciated by Maimonides, each of which begins with the phrase *"Ani Maamin"* ("I believe with perfect faith"). They are existence of God the Creator; unity of God; incorporeality of God; his eternity; that

prayer is meant for God alone; that the Prophets are true; that Moses is supreme above the other Prophets; that the Torah was given to Moses; immutability of the Torah; God's omniscience; divine retribution; belief in the advent of the Messiah; and resurrection of the dead. The principles are found in the prayer book in normal prose, and also in a poetic version (composed in Rome in 1300) incorporated in the Yigdal prayer, which is often the closing song of the Friday night service. Many scholars never accepted the idea of a formal set of dogmas, while others disputed some of the principles. The Jews incarcerated in Nazi concentration camps chanted the principle dealing with the advent of the Messiah to a haunting melody, which is sung to this day.

THREE WEEKS. Mourning period from the 17th of Tammuz, when the walls of Jerusalem were breached, to the 9th of Av, when the Holy Temple was destroyed by the Romans.

TIK. *See* Torah Ornaments.

TIKKUN. Order of service for special occasions, usually recited at night, e.g., for Hoshanah Rabbah, for Shavuoth, and among kabbalistic Jews, every midnight.

TISHA B'AV. 9th day of the Hebrew month Av, the traditional day of the destruction of the First and Second Temple, always regarded by the Talmud as a day when "disasters recurred to the Jewish people." Some claim the expulsion of the Jews from Spain in 1492 began on this day. The day is observed as a fast by all except Reform Jews.

TISHRI. First month of the Jewish year. It includes the High Holy Days and Sukkoth.

TITHE. Ancient form of tax, representing one-tenth of one's produce, to be given to the Levites.

TOCHACHA. (Hebrew for, literally, "rebukes.") Two sections of the Torah contain Moses' admonition to the Israelites to observe God's commandments, warning that failure to do so would bring on drastic punishments. The warnings are read from the Torah in an undertone; today the reader is called to the Torah when this section is read out (everyone else being reluctant to be called when this awesome part is arrived at).

TOMB OF RACHEL. Located in Bethlehem, the tomb of one of the four Matriarchs has for centuries been a place of pilgrimage for Jewish worshipers. The other Matriarchs and the Patriarchs are believed to be buried in Hebron. *See also* Machpelah.

TOMBSTONE. It is customary to erect a tombstone over a grave of a loved one in the 12th month after burial (in Israel, within 30 days, the period of mourning known as sheloshim). Most tombstones today are inscribed in Hebrew and English (or whatever the locality's language is). The tombstone of a Kohen, a priest, is usually decorated with the symbol of the priestly blessing, i.e., two hands extended, with the fingertips touching.

TORAH. (Hebrew for, literally, "teaching" or "guidance.") Generally refers to the Five Books of Moses, also known as the Humash ("Pentateuch"), the first third of the Bible. The term is also used broadly for the whole Bible as well as the oral law; it has also come to mean all of Jewish culture and teaching. Study of Torah has always been considered a fundamental, lifelong obligation, and historians view it as the source of Jewish spiritual strength and survival. *Torah* is sometimes translated as "the law," but the word is misleading inasmuch as the Torah contains not only laws but also history, legend, folklore, and moral and ethical teachings. The scroll of the Law (*Sefer Torah*), which contains a handwritten parchment or vellum transcript of the Pentateuch, read aloud in the synagogue on Sabbath and festivals, is the holiest Jewish religious object.

TORAH ORNAMENTS. A me'il is the mantle that drapes the scroll of the Law; the mappah (or vimpel among German Jews) is the band that ties the two halves together after use; the keter is the crown that adorns the Torah, as do the rimmonim (pl.), pomegranate-shaped tinkling small crowns that fit into the rollers; the hoshen is a breastplate, recalling the breastplate of the High Priest; and a yad, or hand, is a pointer used by the reader to help in the reading, since the scroll contains neither vowels nor punctuation. Among Jews from eastern countries there is also a tik (literally "a case"), a hinged box in which the Torah is kept and from which the reading takes place, with the scroll kept in an upright position.

Set of Ashkenazi Torah ornaments from
Germany comprising mantle, rimmonim, breastplate
and pointer displayed against a parochet.

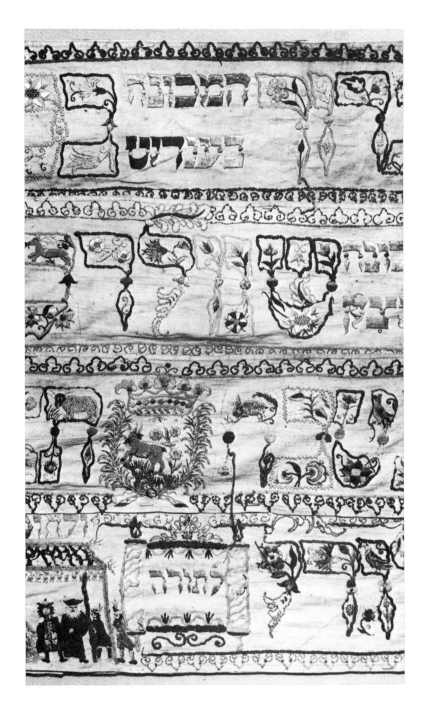

Linen Torah wrapper. Germany, 1738.

Silver Torah case. Persia, 1764.

TOSAFOT. (Hebrew for, "additions.") Refers to outer columns of comments found on all editions of the Talmud, and are additions to the traditional commentary of Rashi. The tosafists, or authors of these comments, originated in northern France (Rashi's home) and their work dated from the 12th to the 14th centuries. Rashi's sons-in-law and grandson were among the best-known tosafists.

TRANSMIGRATION OF SOULS. Belief in life after death, with death seen as a transfer to a new existence. The belief includes the contention that souls can reappear in different people, as well as in beasts, plants, and even stones. The belief was first mentioned by Saadyah, who said he would ordinarily not argue with "foolish" people who held this belief were it not for the fact that he thought them dangerous, since they could influence others. The belief was strong among mystics.

TREE OF LIFE. Term used in the prayer service, denoting the entire spectrum of Judaism.

TROP. Cantillation for the Torah reading. *See also* Accents.

TU B'SHVAT. 15th of Shvat, known as Jewish Arbor Day, when it is customary to plant tree saplings in Israel. (Also known as *Chamisha Asar B'Shvat*.)

TWELVE TRIBES. The twelve tribes of Israel are descended from the twelve sons of Jacob, the third of the Patriarchs of the Jewish people. (Abraham and Isaac are the first and second Patriarchs.) When the ancient Israelites entered the Promised Land, following their flight from bondage in Egypt, each tribe—except Levi —was accorded a section of the land. Levi did not receive any territory inasmuch as the Levites were deemed a priestly tribe, consecrated to worship and teaching. However, the land was still divided into twelve portions, since each of Joseph's sons—Ephraim and Manasseh—received a portion. Thus, there were twelve territorial divisions among the following: Judah, Issachar, Zebulun, Reuben, Simeon, Gad,

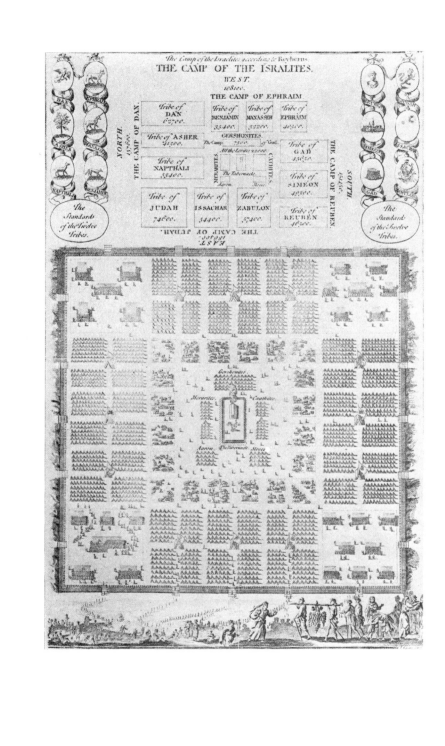

Benjamin, Dan, Naphtali, Asher, Ephraim, Manasseh.

TZA'AR BAALEI HAYIM. Prevention of cruelty to animals, a concept dating back to the Bible. Rabbinic teachings held that a person should not sit down to his meal until he has fed his animals. Cruelty to animals is seen as a Biblical offense.

TZADDIK. Righteous person (based on the word *tzedek*, "justice"). Hasidic Jews refer to their Rebbe or leader as a tzaddik.

TZEDAKAH. *See* Charity.

TZE'ENAH U-RE'ENAH. Yiddish homiletical commentary and explanation of the Torah, written especially for women, and in wide use from the 17th century onward. Jewish housewives often spent Sabbath afternoons reading (and chanting) from the work.

TZITZIT. Biblically prescribed fringes on the four corners of a garment, usually restricted today to the tallit or the tallit katan (also known as arba canfot), a small tallit worn under one's clothes by Orthodox male Jews after the age of 13. There is a set formula for making and knotting the strands so that they conform to Halachah laws.

TZUR ISRAEL. Rock of Israel—a term for God.

UNION OF AMERICAN HEBREW CONGREGATIONS. National organization of Reform temples in the U.S. and Canada.

UNION OF ORTHODOX JEWISH CONGREGATIONS OF AMERICA. National organization of Orthodox synagogues in the U.S. and Canada.

UNITED SYNAGOGUE OF AMERICA. National organization of Conservative synagogues in the U.S. and Canada.

UNLEAVENED BREAD. *See* Matzah.

UNTERFIRER. (Yiddish for "those who escort.")

Used to describe the couple who escort the bride and groom to the huppah or wedding canopy. The honor is usually reserved for the parents, but in their absence is transferred to another married couple.

URIM AND THUMMIM. An oracle in Temple days, attached to the High Priest's breastplate, through which God's will was made known to the people of Israel. The oracle was generally consulted before battle, when the king or judge would ask God, through the High Priest, whether the Israelites would be victorious. The Urim and Thummim were no longer used after the destruction of the First Temple.

USHPIZIN. (Aramaic for "guests.") Usually used today to refer to guests invited to participate in a sukkah meal.

USURY. The Bible forbids charging interest for a loan. The prohibition, however, seems to have been ignored during Biblical times. In view of the economic realities of our own day, but not wishing to blatantly ignore a Biblical command, banks in Israel charge interest through the legal fiction of *hetter iska,* under which a loan is extended in the form of a partnership.

VEGETARIANISM. Judaism has always regarded consumption of animal food as a privilege granted to man because of his superior moral and intellectual gifts. Refraining from eating meat was ordained for mourners until after the funeral, and in periods of national distress or mourning, as in the three weeks or, more commonly, the nine days preceding the 9th of Av fast day. Many Rabbinic commentators expressed the hope that in the Messianic era all people would become vegetarians. Before the Deluge, only fruits and vegetables were permissible foods; afterward, the covenant with Noah permitted man to eat "every moving thing that liveth."

VERSE. Small section of the Bible, usually the equivalent of a sentence. Before the 16th century, verses were marked off by a sign known as a *siluk* or *sof pasuk*. Nowadays verses are numbered, in addition to being punctuated. The scroll of the Law, however, has no punctuation.

VIDUI. *See* Confession.

VIGIL, NIGHT OF. (*Leil shimurim* in Hebrew.) Biblical description of the first night of Passover. In some communities the phrase also refers to the night before the circumcision ceremony, when relatives assemble in the home of the mother for a service for the child's welfare.

VIRTUE. There is no Hebrew word equivalent to the concept of virtue. Moral behavior follows, in Judaism, the practice of the Jewish way of life as ordained by God in the Torah. Certain basic ethical classifications are treated at length in Rabbinic literature, including pride, humility, patience, and contentment.

VOCALIZATION. Hebrew consists of consonants, with a system of vowels placed above, alongside, and below the letters.

VOWS. Declaration whereby a person imposed on himself prohibitions permitted by the Torah. A Bet Din (religious court) could nullify such an oath under certain conditions. The traditional Yom Kippur eve service, the Kol Nidre, is a prayer in which God is asked to void all such vows. (Vows between people, however, can be canceled only by the individuals concerned.) Rabbinic authorities discouraged the taking of vows except when it was done to help rid the individual of bad habits.

WAGES. The Bible commanded an employer to pay the wages of "a hired man" immediately upon completion of work. To protect the laborer, Jewish law teaches that payment in kind is not permissible; however, crediting the workman at a nearby bank or store is acceptable. Prisoners of war are to receive fair wages if made to work, according to Jewish law. In the Jubilee year all debts are canceled, but this does not apply to wages that are owed.

WAILING WALL. *See* Kotel.

WANDERING JEW. Legend from a Christian source. It depicts Jews or a Jew as wandering perpetually, because a Jewish cobbler drove Jesus away when he paused to rest by his door while bearing the cross.

WAR. Both the Bible and the Talmud list a number of laws about warfare designed to establish some degree of law in a situation fraught with peril for all. A war can be *milhemet mitzvah* ("commanded by God") or *milhemet reshut* ("permitted war"). Even a bridegroom can be taken from his chamber for the first kind of war, but the second kind could only be launched by the Sanhedrin's decision, with conscription exemptions detailed in the Torah. Soldiers were excused from the dietary laws in wartime, could take fuel without payment, and could eat produce that had not been tithed.

WASHING OF HANDS. (*Netilat yadayim* in Hebrew.) Jewish law stipulates the washing of one's hands—by pouring water over them—after sleep, after bodily functions, before and after meals, before prayer, and after contact with a corpse. A special blessing accompanies each ablution.

WEEKS, FEAST OF. *See* Shavuoth.

WESTERN WALL. *See* Kotel.

WIDOW. The Bible was especially considerate of widows (and orphans), who had little legal protection in ancient times. A widow can remarry anyone except a High Priest. If her husband dies without leaving any children, she can remarry only after receiving halitzah. She is not allowed to remarry, however, until after three months of widowhood. According to the marriage contract (ketubah), a widow is to be provided with support from her deceased husband's estate so long as she does not remarry. Before she remarries she must complete a settlement of all claims and rights on her late husband's estate.

WIG. (*Sheitl* in Yiddish.) Worn by Orthodox Jewish

women after marriage, since indiscriminate exposure of a woman's hair in public is considered unseemly by the Talmud. Beginning in the 15th century observant women shaved their heads after marriage, thereafter always wearing a sheitl. Modern Orthodox women wear a wig to cover their hair, to which some Rabbinic authorities object on the grounds that the (often attractive) wig violates the spirit of the law.

WILDERNESS GENERATION. Usually used to refer to the Israelites who came out of Egypt and wandered in the desert for 40 years but were not privileged to enter the Holy Land. One kabbalistic commentator said that this generation should be called the "generation of knowledge," since they witnessed God's miraculous deeds in freeing them from bondage, and received the Torah at Sinai.

WILL. Jewish law by and large made a formal will unnecessary since the laws of inheritance were spelled out in the Bible. However, a legator who wished to bequeath certain sums outside his immediate family could do so by writing a will with such a provision; at times, despite Rabbinic opposition, an individual who wished to disinherit a member of his family could do so by disposing of his property during his lifetime.

WINE. Despite the Bible's noting that Noah was a drunkard, and that incest followed a drunken spree by Lot, wine in Jewish tradition is generally looked upon as being wholesome and able to "gladden the heart of man." Wine is therefore used in the weekly kiddush and havdalah ceremonies, and at Passover, weddings, and circumcisions. Wine has a blessing all its own—other fruits being lumped together in one prescribed blessing. Torah is compared to water, while the oral law is termed winelike. Excessive drinking was encouraged on Purim and (to a lesser extent) on Simhat Torah.

WITCHES AND WITCHCRAFT. A Biblical injunction that "thou shalt not suffer a witch to live" indicated the strong Jewish opposition to all forms of witchcraft. Vestiges of superstition and belief in amulets as well as foreign spirits persisted, however, in the Middle Ages.

WITNESS. Every man is required to appear before a court and give honest testimony; whoever refrains from doing so is regarded as a sinner. Witnesses are disqualified from giving testimony in cases affecting their relatives. With certain significant exceptions, women were not eligible to act as witnesses. No one is permitted to testify against himself; circumstantial evidence is ruled out; and in criminal cases at least two witnesses are needed.

WOMEN. As in most societies of the time, Biblical and post-Biblical Jewish life was patriarchal, but in many ways special provision was made for the rights of women. In the Creation story woman is described as an equally valuable counterpart to man. Man and woman were created equally in the image of God, and together were called "man" and formed a single unit. This led Rabbinic authorities to declare that whoever is "not married is not a man." Men and women are subject to the same laws, religious prohibitions, and penalties; both could offer sacrifices in the Temple; respect for father and mother is placed on an equal footing. The founders of the Jewish people include the Matriarchs as well as the Patriarchs. Miriam, Deborah, Hannah, Ruth, and Esther are among many Biblical heroines. Men are nevertheless seen as being active, outgoing, protective, while the virtue of women is concentrated in the home. Thus it is the man who gives the ring in a wedding ceremony, while his wife does the accepting. In modern Israel there is universal suffrage, although many Orthodox synagogues there do not allow women to vote. Jewish tradition sees women as making their influence felt through the strength of their personality and character. Legally women may be kosher slaughterers or circumcisers, but in practice they rarely are. Women are generally exempted from duties tied to a particular time limit, since their principal duty is in the home. Rabbis stressed that a man should "love his wife like himself, and to honor her more than himself," and never hurt her or bring her to tears. A wife, in Talmudic literature, is said to be the "crown of her husband" and indeed she "is his home." Women are said in Jewish tradition to have superior compassion, chastity, piety; they have a primary share in educating the children and keeping their husbands from sinful ways. The Talmud, however, adds that women are prone to curiosity, gossip, superstition, and light-mindedness. In recent generations the sadly neglected education of Jewish women has been greatly improved, and today there are growing numbers of women teaching college Judaica courses, while in the Reform and Reconstructionist Rabbinic seminaries a growing number of women are studying for the Rabbinate.

WORLD TO COME. *See Olam Hazeh, Olam Haba.*

WRITTEN LAW. The Torah, as distinct from the oral law. The former was given to Moses by God; the latter is the interpretations and commentaries of generations of Rabbinic scholars.

YAD. (Hebrew for, literally, "hand.") Pointer used by the reader to help with the reading of the scroll of the Law. The yad is often in the shape of a hand, with the index finger in a pointing position.

YAH. One of the names of God.

YAHRZEIT. Yiddish term referring to the anniversary of the death of a close relative. Traditionally a 24-hour yahrzeit candle is kindled on the eve of the anniversary, and the person observing yahrzeit recites kaddish (the mourner's prayer) in synagogue, where whenever possible he is given the honor of leading the congregation in prayer.

YAMIM NORAIM. Days of awe. The ten days beginning with Rosh Hashanah and ending at the conclusion of Yom Kippur. Also known as the ten days of penitence.

YARMULKE. Skullcap worn by observant Jewish males. In modern Hebrew, also called a kipah.

YESHIVA UNIVERSITY. Principal Orthodox Rabbinic seminary in the U.S., in New York, N.Y. Other

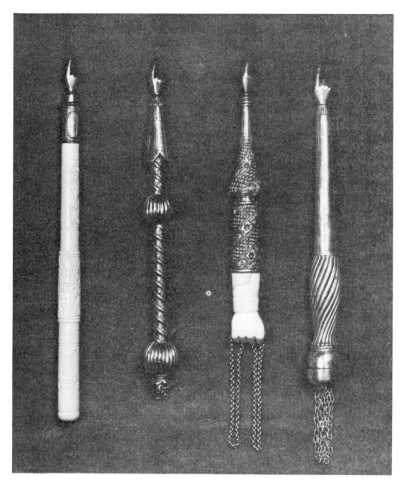

Torah pointers. 1) Pointer with spice box,
United States, 19th Century. 2) Mediterranean,
20th century. 3) Russia, early 19th century.
4) Palestine, 20th century.

Orthodox seminaries are in Baltimore, Md., Skokie, Ill., and Brooklyn, N.Y., in Israel, and in several other countries.

YESHIVAH. Institution for Jewish learning, dating back to ancient times. The modern yeshivah in the U.S. and other western countries is often called a Jewish all-day school, and combines Jewish and secular studies. There are some 100,000 students in American yeshivot (pl.).

YETZER HA-RA, YETZER HA-TOV. (Hebrew for "evil inclination, good inclination.") While the Bible says that man's inclination is "evil from his youth," the Talmud counters that there is an opposing instinct that draws man toward good. Jewish legend sees the former as an evil angel tempting man to evil deeds from the day of birth, which he can overcome only through the study of Torah and the pursuit of good deeds. The opposing angel seeks to persuade man to do good; man has freedom of choice between the two.

YIDDISH. Jewish-German language, with a large sprinkling of Hebrew terms, that became the prime language of the Jews of central and eastern Europe. Including also some Slavic words, the language was invested with a sanctity of its own (written in Hebrew letters), over a period of centuries, and was used by Torah and Talmud students to interpret and comment on the sacred texts. Since the decimation of 6 million Jews in the Nazi Holocaust the language has been on the decline, but pockets of Yiddish-speaking Jews remain in the U.S., Israel, and many other countries.

YIDDISHKEIT. Term that can best be translated as "Jewishness"—denoting the practices and customs of traditional Judaism. It has the additional connotation of Jewish folk traditions and mores.

YIGDAL. Hymn sung at the conclusion of Sabbath eve or Sabbath services. It contains the "13 Articles of Faith" enunciated by Maimonides.

YIHUS. Hebrew word, used equally in Yiddish, referring to distinguished genealogy or connections.

YIMACH SHMO. (Hebrew for "May his name be blotted out.") Curse used after the name of any unremitting enemy of the Jewish people.

YISHAR CO-ACH. Expression of approval and appreciation offered to a Rabbi or cantor after services, or to one who has been called to read the Torah. It may also be used to thank an individual for carrying out a mitzvah. Among the Sephardic Jews the phrase is replaced by "Hazak u'varuch" ("Be strong and blessed").

YIZKOR. Memorial service for the departed, recited

on the three pilgrim festivals (Passover, Shavuoth, Sukkoth) and on the Day of Atonement.

YOM HA-DIN. Day of Judgment. Another name for Yom Kippur.

YOM KIPPUR. Most solemn day of the Jewish religious year, culminating the ten days of awe that began with Rosh Hashanah. Jews spend the entire day in fasting and prayer, soul-searching and repenting for past transgressions, and vowing to lead better lives in the year ahead. Some Jews wear a white kittel at services, and some refrain from wearing leather shoes. It is a day when even the most irreligious Jews make every effort to pass the day according to its rules: in prayer, in repentance, and in pledging charity. On Yom Kippur there is a special closing service, neilah ("locking of the gates"), that is recited on no other day. It refers to the tradition that God writes a person's fate for the New Year on Rosh Hashanah and seals it on Yom Kippur; thus after the neilah service, which concludes the fast day, a man's fate is sealed and set. Not only are food and drink abstained from on Yom Kippur, but sexual intercourse is proscribed. In effect Yom Kippur becomes a full day devoted to prayer and contemplation, transforming the worshiper's day into a period of sanctity that contrasts sharply with the workaday world he is accustomed to. It is interesting that all confessions of sin and transgression recited at services are in the plural, with the congregation praying as a unit, and with virtually all the prayers concentrating on moral and ethical behavior, as opposed to ritual observance.

YOM TOV. Jewish holiday or festival.

Z

ZEMIROT. Hymns sung at the Sabbath table, the melodies having been handed down from generation to generation. Many of the hymns were composed by kabbalists.

ZICHRONO L'VRACHAH. (Hebrew for "May his memory be for a blessing.") Honorific phrase added after the name of a departed person whose memory is held in fond remembrance. In writing the name of the deceased the two Hebrew letters zayin and lamed are added after the name, an abbreviation for the phrase.

ZION. Ancient name for Jerusalem, used today to signify the Jewish state. Some commentators interpret it to mean the spiritual capital of the world. From this word stemmed Zionism, the modern political movement calling for the return to a Jewish national home.

ZOHAR. The chief work of the kabbalah movement, the heart of Jewish mystical teaching, believed to date (in part) from the 2d century.

Appendix

THE HEBREW ALPHABET

Hebrew is one of the oldest languages of mankind. The Hebrew alphabet has undergone several changes in appearance during the past 4,000 years. In modern Hebrew, the vowels are placed above, under, and alongside the 22 consonants comprising the alphabet. Advanced readers of Hebrew do not use vowels, which makes reading a Hebrew newspaper or book difficult for beginners. The prayer book and the Bible are fully voweled.

If you have ever wondered about the similarity between the Hebrew "aleph, bet, gimmel" (the first three letters of the Hebrew alphabet) and the Greek "alpha, beta, gamma" and indeed the similarity of our own A, B, C, there is a simple explanation.

The ancient Israelites, along with the Phoenicians, were a great seafaring people, especially during the reign of King Solomon. They already had in use a code of sounds—in effect, an alphabet—while most other peoples, including the Greeks, did not. The ancient Greeks were impressed by their invention, adapted it (adding some sounds and letters), and in the course of time the Romans adapted it from the Greeks.

After the Jews were exiled from their homeland some 2,000 years ago, their use of Hebrew was limited mostly to prayer, biblical study, and, for a time, religious poetry and philosophy. As a day-to-day spoken and written language, Hebrew lay dormant, although the various "Jewish" languages (Yiddish, Ladino and others) developed during the two-millenial Diaspora and continued to use Hebrew letters.

Toward the end of the nineteenth century, a man called Eliezer Ben Yehudah said to his friends and colleagues that the rebirth of the ancient language was essential to the success of the movement to restore the Jews to their homeland, i.e., Zionism. A zealot for Hebrew, he coined numerous new words, basing them largely on roots found in the Bible and Talmud, and created a modern dictionary. As a result of his determination, Hebrew gradually began to be used on a daily basis among the Jews resettling in Palestine, and today it is of course the principal, official language of Israel.

In the early decades of America, Hebrew was studied avidly in the fledgling universities, and commencement speakers at Harvard and Yale were actually required to deliver their talks in Hebrew. The language is taught today in numerous colleges and universities throughout the world (as well as in all Jewish schools, of course), and continues to add new terms to its vocabulary, particularly in the sciences, as the need arises.

Hebrew has 22 consonants (five of which change appearance when they end a word). Vowels are placed above, below, and alongside the letters. Shown here is the Hebrew alphabet, with the name of each letter and the equivalent English sound.

א	aleph	"a" sound	ל	lamed	"l" sound
ב	beth	"b" sound	מ ם	mem	"m" sound
ג	gimel	"g" (hard) sound	נ ן	nun	"n" sound
			ס	samech	"s" sound
ד	daled	"d" sound	ע	ayin	"a" sound
ה	hay	"h" sound	פ ף	pay	"p" sound
ו	vav	"v" sound	צ ץ	tsadi	"ts" sound
ז	zayin	"z" sound	ק	kof	"k" sound
ח	het	"ch" (guttural) sound	ר	resh	"r" sound
			שׁ	shin	"sh" sound
ט	tet	"t" sound	שׂ	śin	"s" sound
י	yod	"y" sound	ת	tav	"t" sound
כ ך	caf	"k" sound			

The letters that change appearance at the end of a word are Caf (without the dot, it is pronounced "chaf," a guttural), Mem, Nun, Pay (without the dot, it becomes "Fay," an "F" sound), and Tsadi.

By removing the dot from the Bet, the sound changes to "V;" by shifting the dot on the Shin from right to left, the sound becomes "S." The dot can also be removed from the Tet but in modern, Israel-version Hebrew, the sound of "T" does not change.

The letters are also used numerically, i.e., each letter represents a number, and a combination of letters equals various numerical figures. Thus, for example, the traditional figure used for the Jewish year (beginning in September 1977) is shown in four Hebrew letters ה׳תשל״ח , and stands for 5,738. This is arrived at as follows:

The letter ה or five is understood to mean 5,000.

The letter ת is 400. The letter ש is 300. The letter ל is 30. The letter ח is 8. When you total them, you arrive at 738.

This alphabetical-numerical system is known as Gematriah and to this day, among those inclined to mysticism, various words and phrases are interpreted numerically, to indicate that a given happy or tragic event will soon occur.

The basic method of counting numerically follows:

א = 1	יא = 11	ל = 30
ב = 2	יב = 12	מ = 40
ג = 3	יג = 13	נ = 50
ד = 4	יד = 14	ס = 60
ה = 5	טו = 15	ע = 70
ו = 6	טז = 16	פ = 80
ז = 7	יז = 17	צ = 90
ח = 8	יח = 18	ק = 100
ט = 9	יט = 19	ר = 200
י = 10	כ = 20	ש = 300
		ת = 400

DAYS OF THE WEEK

The six days of the week are known by their numerical names:

Yom rishon (literally, first day) is Sunday.

Yom sheni (second day), Monday.

Yom shlishi (third day), Tuesday.

Yom r'vi'i (fourth day), Wednesday.

Yom chamishi (fifth day), Thursday.

Yom shishi (sixth day), Friday.

Sabbath, known in Hebrew as Shabbat (and in Yiddish as Shabbes), is the seventh day of the week and is set aside as a day of rest, prayer, and study. Observance of the Sabbath is ordained in the Ten Commandments. (See entry p. 162.)

As with all Jewish holidays and festivals, the Sabbath begins on the eve of the preceding day and is therefore known as *Erev Shabbat* or Sabbath eve.

MONTHS OF THE YEAR

The Hebrew months of the year are: Tishrei, Heshvan, Kislev, Tevet, Sh'vat, Adar, Nissan, Iyar, Sivan, Tammuz, Av, Elul.

Most years have 353, 354, or 355 days but during a leap year an additional 30 days are added. The month of Adar is "doubled," i.e., there is an Adar I and an Adar II.

The month of Heshvan is also known as Marheshvan, or "bitter Heshvan," because there is no Jewish holiday or festival occurring throughout the month.

Tishrei is a busy holiday month: Rosh Hashanah falls on the first and second days of the month (usually in September); Yom Kippur on the tenth day; and the Sukkot-Simhat Torah holidays are observed from the 15th through the 23rd days of the month.

Chanukkah (often spelled Hanukkah) begins on the 25th of Kislev and lasts eight days.

Jewish Arbor Day, known as Tu B'Sh'vat or Chamisha Asar B'Shvat, falls on the 15th day of Sh'vat.

On the 14th of Adar, Purim is celebrated. The first day of Passover falls on the 15th of Nissan. In recent years, a new date has been marked on the Jewish calendar—the 27th of Nissan, Remembrance Day, honoring the memory of the six million Jews who were murdered during the Nazi era.

Iyar is marked by Israel Independence Day, on the 5th day (in 1978, Israel will mark its 30th anniversary), and Lag B'Omer, on the 18th day.

Shavuoth begins on the 6th day of Sivan, and the 9th day of Av is a day of mourning for the destruction of the Holy Temples, first in 586 B.C.E. and a second time in 70 C.E.

The month of Elul is traditionally a period when Jews visit the graves of their loved ones, since it precedes the oncoming High Holy Days of Rosh Hashanah and Yom Kippur.

MAJOR JEWISH HOLIDAYS
AND FESTIVALS

	1979	1980	1981
Rosh Hashanah	Sept. 22	Sept. 11	Sept. 29
Yom Kippur	Oct. 1	Sept. 20	Oct. 8
Sukkot	Oct. 6	Sept. 25	Oct. 13
Simhat Torah	Oct. 14	Oct. 3	Oct. 21
Hanukkah	Dec. 15	Dec. 3	Dec. 21
Tu B'Shvat	Feb. 13	Feb. 2	Jan. 20
Purim	Mar. 13	Mar. 2	Mar. 20
Passover	Apr. 12	Apr. 1	Apr. 19
Remembrance Day	Apr. 24	Apr. 27	May 1
Israel Independence Day	May 1	Apr. 20	May 8
Shavuoth	June 1	May 21	June 8
Tisha B'Av	Aug. 2	July 22	Aug. 9

1982	1983	1984	1985	1986
Sept. 18	Sept. 8	Sept. 27	Sept. 16	Oct. 4
Sept. 27	Sept. 17	Oct. 6	Sept. 25	Oct. 13
Oct. 2	Sept. 22	Oct. 11	Sept. 30	Oct. 18
Oct. 10	Sept. 30	Oct. 19	Oct. 8	Oct. 26
Dec. 11	Dec. 1	Dec. 19	Dec. 8	Dec. 27
Feb. 8	Jan. 30	Jan. 19	Feb. 6	Jan. 25
Mar. 9	Feb. 27	Mar. 18	Mar. 7	Mar. 25
Apr. 8	Mar. 29	Apr. 17	Apr. 6	Apr. 24
Apr. 20	Apr. 10	Apr. 29	Apr. 18	May 6
Apr. 27	Apr. 17	May 6	Apr. 25	May 13
May 28	May 18	June 6	May 26	June 13
July 29	July 19	Aug. 7	July 27	Aug. 14

MAJOR DATES IN JEWISH HISTORY

1800 B.C.E.	Abraham introduces the concept of monotheism, and receives God's promise that the children of Israel will receive the land of Canaan as an eternal inheritance.
1440 B.C.E.	Israelites flee from Egyptian slavery, and receive the Ten Commandments at Mount Sinai.
1000 B.C.E.	King David comes to power, and the first Holy Temple is built by David's son, King Solomon.
586 B.C.E.	First Holy Temple is destroyed by Babylonians, and the majority of Jews are exiled.
515 B.C.E.	Destroyed Temple is rebuilt. Ten of original twelve tribes are lost forever.
165 B.C.E.	Maccabees lead revolt against the Romans, who control the Jewish homeland, thereby cleansing Temple of pagan worship. Origin of Chanukkah festival.
70 C.E.	Second Holy Temple destroyed by the Romans, majority of Jews are exiled.
200 C.E.	Rabbi Judah HaNassi assembles the Oral Law, the Mishnah, and records it for permanent use.
500 C.E.	Compilation and recording of Babylonian Talmud is completed.
950 C.E.	Spain emerges as center of Golden Age of Jewish learning, producing such giants as Halevi, Ibn Gabirol, Ibn Ezra, and Maimonides.
1096–1492 C.E.	Crusades sweep the European Jewish communities, causing untold hardship. In this period, Jews

are expelled from England and France, and in 1492, the Jews of Spain are ordered to leave the country.

1654 c.e.   Handful of Jews, fleeing from persecution in Brazil, reach New Amsterdam, where they are reluctantly given asylum.

1789 c.e.   French revolution ushers in a new era of emancipation for Jews in western Europe.

1861 c.e.   Early Zionist settlements begin to appear in Palestine, as Jewish national homeland movement begins to develop.

1881 c.e.   Anti-Semitic legislation in Czarist Russia sets off large-scale East European Jewish migration to the U.S.

1917 c.e.   British issue Balfour Declaration, promising establishment of Jewish homeland in Palestine.

1920–28 c.e.   Rising anti-Semitism in Europe accelerates migration of Jews to Palestine, the U.S. and Latin America.

1933 c.e.   Nazi era begins, with Jews marked as objects for destruction.

1939–45 c.e.   World War II sees one-third of world's Jewish community—six million Jews—murdered in implementation of Nazi program to annihilate all Jews.

1948 c.e.   State of Israel proclaims independence, wins immediate recognition by U.S. and defeats attacks of neighboring Arab countries.

Note: b.c.e., Before Common Era
    c.e., Common Era

JEWISH POPULATION FIGURES

The most recent figures available on Jewish demography follow:

Total world Jewish population: 14,145,000.

U.S. Jewish population: 5,845,000, equal to 2.7 percent of total population.

Israel's Jewish population, 3,000,000; U.S.S.R., 2,675,000; France, 550,000; Britain, 410,000; Canada, 305,000; Argentina, 300,000.

Major concentrations of Jews in the U.S.: Greater N.Y., 2,000,000; Los Angeles, 455,000; Philadelphia, 350,000; Chicago, 250,000 Miami, 225,000; Boston, 180,000; Washington, D.C., 112,500; Bergen County, N.J., 100,000; Essex County, N.J., 95,000; Baltimore, 92,000; Cleveland, 80,000; Detroit, 80,000; San Francisco, 75,000; St. Louis, 60,000; Montgomery County, Md., 50,000.

Other Jewish population figures for European and Latin American countries, selected at random: Ireland, 4,000; Belgium, 40,000; Yugoslavia, 6,000; Rumania, 60,000; Hungary, 80,000; Switzerland, 21,000; Italy, 35,000; Brazil, 165,000; Uruguay, 50,000; Mexico, 37,500; Peru, 6,000.

Some major world cities and their Jewish populations (excluding U.S.) follow: Tel Aviv, 400,000; Teheran, 50,000; Toronto, 110,000; Sao Paulo, 65,000; Melbourne, 34,000; Istanbul, 22,000; Kiev, 170,000; Leningrad, 165,000; Paris, 300,000; Rome, 15,000; Marseilles, 65,000; Johannesburg, 63,000; Jerusalem, 266,000.

ISRAEL'S FORM OF GOVERNMENT

Israel is a democracy in which the supreme authority rests with the Knesset (Parliament), a single-chamber legislative body consisting of 120 members. The Knesset is elected by universal suffrage for four years, but can decide to hold earlier elections by passages of suitable legislation. The system of proportional legislation is used, i.e., voters choose a particular party and the number of seats allocated to the party is determined by the total number of ballots cast.

A president is elected for a period of five years by the Knesset. The president in turn appoints the members of the Judiciary, from the lowest magistrate courts to the Supreme Court. The president's role is largely ornamental. Executive power is held by the cabinet and its prime minister, who are responsible to the Knesset. The various cabinet ministers are responsible for specific executive functions, e.g., defense, foreign affairs, agriculture, commerce and industry, police, etc.

Responsible to the Knesset directly is the state comptroller, who is in effect a Commissioner of Public Complaints.

Debates in the Knesset are conducted in Hebrew with simultaneous translations available to Arab members, who also have the right to address the chamber in Arabic. Sessions are open to the public.

Since the establishment of Israel, no single party has achieved an absolute majority, necessitating governance by coalitions.

In its Declaration of Independence of May 1948, Israel promised to "ensure complete equality of social and political rights to all its citizens irrespective of religion, race, or sex. It guarantees freedom of religion, conscience, language, education and culture, and safeguards the holy places of all religions." In addition to some 3,000,000 Jews, Israel is home to about a half-million non-Jews, including Moslems, Christians, Druze, Baha'i, Karaites, Samaritans. (The latter two are Jewish sects, small in number; the majority of non-Jews in Israel are Moslems.) The Israel government pays the salaries of some 200 Moslem clergymen, and partly finances the salaries of rabbis and other religious functionaries.

Israel has some 6,000 synagogues (some of them quite small), 90 mosques, 300 churches and chapels, as well as other houses of worship. The world headquarters and chief shrines of the Baha'i faith are found in Haifa and Acre.

Suggested Reading List

Authorized Daily Prayerbook, Hertz. New York: Bloch Publishing Co.

Pentateuch and Haftarahs, Hertz. London: Soncino Press.

Code of Jewish Law (annotated ed.), Ganzfried. New York: Hebrew Publishing Co.

Jewish Worship, Millgram. Philadelphia: Jewish Publication Society of America.

For the Sake of Heaven, Buber. New York: Schocken Books.

Judaism and Modern Man, Herberg. New York: Schocken Books.

Man Is Not Alone, Heschel. New York: Farrar, Straus & Giroux.

A Book of Jewish Concepts, Birnbaum. New York: Hebrew Publishing Co.

Judaic Tradition, Glatzer, ed. Boston: Beacon Press.

The Jews, Finkelstein. New York: Schocken Books.

Lifetime of a Jew, Schauss. New York: Union of American Hebrew Congregations.

Maimonides Reader, Twersky, ed. New York: Behrman House.

Jewish Theology, Jacobs. New York: Behrman House.

Aspects of Rabbinic Theology, Schechter. New York: Schocken Books.

Crisis and Faith, Berkovits. New York: Hebrew Publishing Co.

Introduction to Talmud and Midrash, Strack. New York: Schocken Books.

To Be A Jew, Donin. New York: Basic Books.

Faith of Judaism, Epstein. London: Soncino Press.

This Is My God, Wouk. New York: Doubleday.

The Jewish Catalog, Strassfeld, et al., eds. Philadelphia: Jewish Publication Society of America.

Photo Credits

LIBRARY OF THE JEWISH THEOLOGICAL SEMINARY OF AMERICA pages 5, 12, 36 (photo by Tita Bind), 43, 88, 109 and 155.

YIVO INSTITUTE OF JEWISH RESEARCH pages 11, 24, 62 and 135.

YESHIVA UNIVERSITY MUSEUM PHOTOGRAPHY ARCHIVES pages 15, 20 (Bezalel National Art Museum), 51 (The Albright Institute of Archeological Research) and 137.

COLLECTION OF THE JEWISH MUSEUM, NEW YORK pages 79, 91, 115, 129; page 18 gift of Norman F. Goetz; page 65 gift of Clara Durlacher; pages 94, 112, 113, 114, 121, 123, 140 *top right*, 140 *bottom*, 144, 148, 162, 168 and 178 gifts of Dr. Harry G. Friedman; page 128 gift of Milton J. Bluestein and Jack R. Aron; page 129 *top* gift of Dorothy Bernard; page 129 *bottom* gift of Stafford Lorie; page 140 *top left* from Samuel and Lucille Lemberg Collection; page 151 gift of Rose Mintz; page 158 gift of Rebecca C. Angell; page 167 from the Danzig Community.

CULVER PICTURES pages 26 and 149.

SIR ISAAC AND LADY WOLFSON MUSEUM IN HECHAL SHLOMO pages 34 (photo by David Harris).

THE ISRAEL MUSEUM pages 48 and 103 (Feuchtwanger Collection), 84, 166 (photo by David Harris).

NEW YORK PUBLIC LIBRARY pages 57 and 170.

JOHN RYLANDS LIBRARY, MANCHESTER page 85.

ISRAEL MINISTRY OF TOURISM pages 105.

STATE JEWISH MUSEUM, PRAGUE page 126.

THE BRITISH MUSEUM page 127.